REVISE AQA GCSE (9–1)
Spanish
REVISION GUIDE

Series Consultant: Harry Smith

Author: Vivien Halksworth

Also available to support your revision:

Revise GCSE Study Skills Guide   9781292318875

The **Revise GCSE Study Skills Guide** is full of tried-and-trusted hints and tips for how to learn more effectively. It gives you techniques to help you achieve your best – throughout your GCSE studies and beyond!

Revise GCSE Revision Planner   9781292318868

The **Revise GCSE Revision Planner** helps you to plan and organise your time, step-by-step, throughout your GCSE revision. Use this book and wall chart to mastermind your revision.

Difficulty scale

The scale next to each exam-style question tells you how difficult it is.

Some questions cover a range of difficulties.

The more of the scale that is shaded, the harder the question is.

 Some questions are Foundation level.

Some questions are Higher level.

Some questions are applicable to both levels.

For the full range of Pearson revision titles across KS2, 11+, KS3, GCSE, Functional Skills, AS/A Level and BTEC visit:
www.pearsonschools.co.uk/revise

Contents

AUDIO

Audio files and transcripts for the listening exercises in this book can be accessed by using the QR codes throughout the book, or going to www.pearsonschools.co.uk/mflrevisionaudio.

Listen to the recording

A small bit of small print:
AQA publishes Sample Assessment Material and the Specification on its website. This is the official content and this book should be used in conjunction with it. The questions in 'Now try this' have been written to help you practise every topic in the book. Remember: the real exam questions may not look like this.

Physical descriptions

Describe yourself and your friends successfully by using adjectives correctly.

Cómo soy

¿Cómo eres?   What do you look like?

Tengo el pelo ...   I have ... hair.

rubio y largo   castaño y rizado   negro y corto

Es pelirrojo/a.	He / She has red hair.
Tiene los ojos ...	He / She has ... eyes.
azules / marrones / verdes.	blue / brown / green
Lleva gafas.	He / She wears glasses.
Es calvo.	He is bald.
Es gorda / delgada.	She is fat / slim.
Es guapo / feo.	He is good-looking / ugly.
Soy alto/a / bajo/a.	I'm tall / short.
Tengo / Llevo barba / bigote.	I have a beard / moustache.
Tengo / Llevo un piercing.	I have a body piercing.

Adjectival agreement

Adjectives describe nouns. They must agree with the noun in gender (masculine or feminine) and number (singular or plural).

Grammar page 83

	Singular	Plural
Adjectives ending -o:		
Masculine	alto	altos
Feminine	alta	altas
Adjectives ending in a consonant:		
Masculine	azul	azules
Feminine	azul	azules

Remember: when you're describing hair and eyes, the adjectives need to agree with **pelo** and **ojos**, not with the gender of the person being described.

Worked example

READING

Read the descriptions of four people.

> Tengo los ojos marrones y el pelo negro. Soy un poco gordo. Mi amiga Begoña es bastante alta y tiene el pelo muy corto y castaño. ¡Me encanta su pelo! **Antonio**

> Tengo los ojos azules y el pelo rubio. No soy alto. Mi amiga Daniela es demasiado alta. No lleva gafas y tiene unos piercings que no me gustan. **Pedro**

Who is this? Write the correct letter in each box.

A	Antonio
B	Begoña
C	Pedro
D	Daniela

(a) I am short.   C

(b) I have brown hair.   B

Quantifiers

Use **quantifiers** to extend your sentences and make them more interesting. Antonio and Pedro have used muy (very), bastante (quite), un poco (a little) and demasiado (too). Quantifiers are positioned before the adjective and never change their endings.

Es demasiado alta.   She is **too** tall.

Pay attention to the gender of the adjectives used in these texts, so you know whether they are describing a boy or a girl.

Now try this

READING

Read the texts from the worked example again. Who is this? Write the correct letter in each box.

(a) I am not slim. ☐ **(1 mark)**   (d) I have lovely, short hair. ☐ **(1 mark)**

(b) I do not wear glasses. ☐ **(1 mark)**   (e) I have dark hair and eyes. ☐ **(1 mark)**

(c) I don't like my friend's appearance. ☐ **(1 mark)**

Character descriptions

Describe positive and negative aspects of personality with the verb ser.

¿Cómo es su personalidad?

Es ...   He / She is ...

amistoso/a	friendly
encantador/a	charming
hablador/a	chatty
leal	loyal
optimista	optimistic
simpático/a	likeable, nice

antipático/a	unpleasant
avaro/a	mean, miserly
egoísta	selfish
perezoso/a	lazy
pesimista	pessimistic
travieso/a	naughty

Soy simpática.
I'm likeable.

Soy tonto.
I'm silly.

Soy inteligente.
I'm intelligent.

Soy serio.
I'm serious.

The verb ser (to be)

Grammar page 91

You need to be able to use ser in the present tense to describe characteristics.

Mi hermano es perezoso.   My brother is lazy.

Mis primos son habladores.   My cousins are chatty.

Aiming higher

Use a wider range of **vocabulary and verb forms** to create more complex sentences.
Mi compañero es bastante atrevido y yo estoy un poco loco pero también somos muy responsables.

Try to mention some of these more interesting characteristics.

atrevido/a	daring, cheeky
callado/a	quiet
celoso/a	jealous
comprensivo/a	understanding
loco/a	crazy
maleducado/a	rude
molesto/a	annoying
responsable	responsible
sensato/a	sensible
sensible	sensitive

Worked example

- ¿Cómo es tu personalidad?

  Soy bastante seria y muy simpática. A veces soy habladora, pero nunca soy egoísta.

AIMING HIGHER En mi opinión, soy bastante sensato y creo que también soy muy amistoso. No obstante, no estoy muy seguro de mí mismo y puedo ser un poco tímido. Cuando era pequeño, era muy travieso y un poco avaro con mis hermanos.

Remember to use the correct adjective endings. Here a girl is describing herself, and in the next paragraph it is a boy speaking.

Using exciting adjectives such as **sensato** and **amistoso** makes this answer more interesting. By saying **puedo ser un poco tímido** (I can be a little shy) the student shows understanding of how to use infinitives. Also, talking about the past in **era muy travieso** demonstrates knowledge of the imperfect tense.

Now try this

Answer this question using at least three long sentences.
- ¿Cómo es tu personalidad?

Describing family

You often need to talk about your own family.

¿Cómo es tu familia?

Me parezco a mi hermano menor / mayor.
I look like my younger / older brother.
Me llevo bien con mis primos.
I get on well with my cousins.
Me llevo mal con mi hermanastra.
I don't get on well with my stepsister.

padre   abuelo   madre   abuela

hijo   hija

mi madrastra	my stepmother
mi padrastro	my stepfather
mi tío / tía	my uncle / aunt
su marido, su esposo	her husband
su mujer, su esposa	his wife

Possessive adjectives

Grammar page 84

Possessive adjectives agree with the noun they describe, not the person who 'possesses'.

	m.sing.	f.sing.	m.pl.	f.pl.
my	mi	mi	mis	mis
your (sing.)	tu	tu	tus	tus
his/her/its	su	su	sus	sus
our	nuestro	nuestra	nuestros	nuestras
your (pl.)	vuestro	vuestra	vuestros	vuestras
their	su	su	sus	sus

Mis padres están divorciados.
My parents are divorced.
Nuestros padres están separados.
Our parents are separated.
Sus padres están casados.
His/Her/Their parents are married.

If using the politc / formal form of 'you' (usted – polite singular; ustedes – polite plural), use su / sus for 'your'.

Worked example

🎧 LISTENING TRACK 1

Listen to Carmen. Put the correct letter in the box.
Según Carmen, es importante …

Listen to the recording

A	compartir cosas con su familia
B	tener padres que estén casados
C	ver a sus padres cada día

[A]   **(1 mark)**

– Para mí, pasar tiempo con tus parientes es importante.

Exam alert

When the multiple-choice questions are in Spanish, read them carefully and try to work out what they mean before you hear the recording. You may not remember that compartir means 'to share', but you can get the gist by understanding that con tu familia means 'with your family'.

To answer this question correctly, you need to know that **parientes** is a false friend: it means 'relatives', **not** 'parents'.

Now try this

🎧 LISTENING TRACK 2

Listen to Carmen talking more about her family. Put the correct letter in the box.
Carmen tiene una mala relación con …

Listen to the recording

A	su madre.
B	su padre.
C	sus parientes.

☐

Remember to read all the options carefully before you listen.

(1 mark)

Friends

You can use this page to prepare your thoughts about friends and friendship.

Los amigos

Un buen amigo debe ...	A good friend must ...
saber escuchar.	know how to listen.
ayudarte con tus problemas.	help you with your problems.
decirte la verdad.	tell you the truth.
estar siempre a tu lado.	always be by your side.
recordar tu cumpleaños.	remember your birthday.
ser como un hermano.	be like a brother.
aceptarte como eres.	accept you as you are.

Creo que los amigos son importantes.
I think friends are important.

Es importante que los amigos se lleven bien.
It's important that friends get on well.

Los amigos están ahí para apoyarte.
Friends are there to support you.

La amistad es más importante que el amor.
Friendship is more important than love.

The verbs deber and saber

	deber – to have to, must	saber – to know (information)
I	debo	sé
you (sing.)	debes	sabes
he/she/it	debe	sabe
we	debemos	sabemos
you (pl.)	debéis	sabéis
they	deben	saben

Un buen amigo debería ser leal.
A good friend should be loyal.

Un buen amigo sabe guardar tus secretos.
A good friend knows how to keep your secrets.

Worked example

Opinion words (en mi opinión, creo que) can improve your communication and content.

¿Cómo es un buen amigo?

> En mi opinión, un buen amigo debe estar siempre a tu lado y saber guardar tus secretos. Debe aceptarte como eres. Creo que los amigos son importantes.

Comparatives (es más importante que) show a confident use of more complex structures. Subjunctive clauses (se lleven bien after es esencial que ...) show more complex language handled confidently.

AIMING HIGHER

> En mi opinión, los amigos están ahí para apoyarte; no siempre están a tu lado, pero pueden guardar tus secretos. Deben aceptarte como eres. Creo que los amigos son tan importantes como la familia. Es esencial que los amigos se lleven bien. A mi parecer, la amistad es más importante que el amor.

Exam alert

In the speaking exam, you can use the preparation time to make notes on what you want to say, but you mustn't prepare whole sentences and then just read them out.

Now try this

Include **connectives** to make your work more coherent and fluent.

Answer the question in 30–40 seconds.
• ¿Cómo es un buen amigo?

Relationships

Be prepared to understand texts about relationships and to talk about them.

Las relaciones

¿Quieres salir el viernes?
Do you want to go out on Friday?

No puedo, estoy ocupado.
I can't, I'm busy.

Sí, podemos ir a la fiesta.
Yes, we can go to the party.

Conocí a mi novio en el instituto.
I met my boyfriend at school.

estar enamorado/a de	to be in love with
depender de	to depend on
contar con	to rely on
sentirse feliz	to feel happy

Rompí con mi novia.
I broke up with my girlfriend.

estar solo/a	to be alone
discutimos mucho	we argue a lot
a veces nos peleamos	sometimes we fight
sentirse triste	to feel sad

Radical-changing verbs

Grammar page 88

In radical-changing verbs, the vowel in the first syllable changes in the singular and third person plural.

	poder – to be able	querer – to want
I	puedo	quiero
you	puedes	quieres
he / she / it	puede	quiere
we	podemos	queremos
you	podéis	queréis
they	pueden	quieren

Poder and querer are followed by the infinitive:

No puedo salir.   I can't go out.

¿Quiere ir al cine el viernes?   Does he want to go to the cinema on Friday?

Worked example

READING

Read this extract from the play *Bodas de sangre* by Federico García Lorca where the bridegroom's mother is trying to find out about her son's girlfriend.

Vecina: Tienes razón. Tu hijo vale mucho.
Madre: Vale. Por eso lo cuido. A mí me habían dicho que la muchacha (chica) tuvo novio hace tiempo.
Vecina: Tendría ella quince años. Él se casó ya hace dos años con una prima de ella, por cierto. Nadie se acuerda del noviazgo.
Madre: ¿Cómo te acuerdas tú?
Vecina: ¡Me haces unas preguntas...!
Madre: A cada uno le gusta enterarse de lo que le duele. ¿Quién fue el novio?
Vecina: Leonardo.
Madre: ¿Qué Leonardo?
Vecina: Leonardo, el de los Félix.
Madre: (Levantándose) ¡De los Félix!
Vecina: Mujer, ¿qué culpa tiene Leonardo de nada? Él tenía ocho años cuando las cuestiones.
Madre: Es verdad... Pero oigo eso de Félix y es lo mismo.

Answer the following question **in English**.

What rumour is the mother concerned about?   **(1 mark)**

That the girl had a boyfriend/fiancé before.

Reading literary texts strategies

✓ If you are given an introduction that sets the scene, always read it. It can really help you understand the context of the extract.

✓ There will be words that you don't recognise or haven't seen before. Don't worry. Use the words and structures that you do know to help you work them out.

The question mentions a rumour, so the verb **me habían dicho**, meaning 'they had told me' suggests that what follows must be the rumour she has heard. **Tuvo novio** means 'she had a boyfriend' and **hace tiempo** means 'a while ago'.

Now try this

READING

Read the extract in the worked example again. Answer the following questions **in English**.

(a) What age would the girl have been when she had her previous boyfriend/fiancé?   **(1 mark)**

(b) What became of the old boyfriend/fiancé?   **(1 mark)**

(c) When did this happen?   **(1 mark)**

(d) What information makes the mother jump up with shock?   **(1 mark)**

Marriage and partnership

Revise vocabulary and phrases to express your views about relationships.

El matrimonio y las relaciones

el amor	love
el beso	kiss
la boda	wedding
el compromiso	engagement
casarse (con)	to get married (to)
estar casado/a	to be married
estar soltero/a	to be single
el casamiento	marriage, wedding
el matrimonio	marriage, married couple
enamorarse de	to fall in love with
la felicidad	happiness
el novio / la novia	boyfriend / girlfriend
la pareja	couple
el marido / el esposo	husband
la mujer / la esposa	wife
la igualdad	equality
la confianza	confidence, trust
la independencia	independence
celoso/a	jealous
cariñoso/a	affectionate
discutir	to argue
pelear(se)	to fight
separarse	to separate
divorciarse	to get divorced
estar divorciado/a	to be divorced

Ser and estar

Ser is used when the next word is a noun:
Pablo es mi novio.
Pablo is my boyfriend.
Ser is also used with an adjective that describes a quality or characteristic of a permanent nature (one that will not change overnight):
Elena es muy celosa.   Elena is very jealous.   (i.e. she is the jealous type).

Estar is used to say where someone or something is:
Mi marido está en Madrid.
My husband is in Madrid.

Estar is also used with an adjective that describes a temporary condition or state:
Estás muy cariñoso hoy.
You're very affectionate today.

Estar is also used with casado, divorciado, soltero and separado.

Worked example

Tu amigo español quiere saber tus planes para el futuro.
Escríbele tus ideas sobre el matrimonio y las relaciones.
Menciona:
- la edad ideal para casarse
- cómo es el novio / la novia ideal.

Escribe aproximadamente 45 palabras **en español**.   **(8 marks)**

En mi opinión, no es una buena idea casarse muy joven. Me gustaría casarme a los veintiocho años, más o menos. Mi novia ideal tendría buen sentido del humor y sería simpática y comprensiva. Siempre sería cariñosa y nunca sería celosa.

Aiming higher

Find one magazine article aimed at teenagers and read it. Look up and jot down any vocabulary that you don't know. This will help you to get used to more complex texts – by breaking them down into smaller chunks they become much easier to read!

Make sure you are familiar with future and conditional tenses for this topic as you will be talking about what you will do or would do in the future.

Now try this

Write your own response to the bullet points in the worked example. Write about **45** words **in Spanish**.   **(8 marks)**

When I was younger

Use the imperfect tense to describe what you did when you were younger.

Cuando era pequeño

Cuando era pequeño me gustaban los osos de peluche. When I was younger I liked teddy bears.

Cuando era pequeño ... | When I was younger ...
- disfrutaba explorar. — I enjoyed exploring.
- me encantaban los dibujos animados. — I loved cartoons.
- jugaba en mi habitación. — I used to play in my room.
- comía caramelos. — I ate sweets.
- bebía más leche. — I drank more milk.
- montaba en bici en el parque — I rode my bike in the park.
- me subía a los árboles. — I climbed trees.
- era tan inocente. — I was so innocent.
- no era travieso/a. — I wasn't naughty.

Cuando éramos pequeños ... | When we were younger ...
- mi familia y yo comíamos juntos. — my family and I ate together.
- leíamos muchos tebeos. — we read lots of comics.
- jugábamos al ajedrez. — we played chess.
- queríamos ser mayores. — we wanted to be grown-up.
- nunca nos aburríamos. — we were never bored.

Imperfect tense

Grammar page 94

The imperfect tense is used to describe what **used to happen** or what **was happening**.
It is formed as follows:

hablar to speak, talk	comer to eat	vivir to live
hablaba	comía	vivía
hablabas	comías	vivías
hablaba	comía	vivía
hablábamos	comíamos	vivíamos
hablabais	comíais	vivíais
hablaban	comían	vivían

Use these **time expressions** to add detail to sentences you write with the imperfect tense.
A menudo nos reuníamos.
We **often** got together.
Mi madre siempre cocinaba.
My mum **always** used to cook.
Nunca ordenaba mi habitación.
I **never** tidied my room.
A veces cantaba canciones pop con mis amigos.
Sometimes I would sing pop songs with my friends.

Worked example

An actor is talking about his childhood. Listen and answer the following question **in English**.
What was good about his family?   **(1 mark)**

His sisters loved doing the same things as him.

Listen to the recording

– Cuando era pequeño era muy travieso. Tenía dos hermanas igual de traviesas y nos encantaba hacer las mismas cosas.

The text begins in the imperfect tense (**Cuando era pequeño**), so you know the man is describing his past experiences.
The question asks you about his family, so you should be listening out for any family members, not just the word **familia**. He talks about his sisters (**hermanas**).
When the question asks about a positive aspect of something, remember to listen out for any opinions mentioned. He says **nos encantaba**.

Now try this

Listen to the whole recording from the worked example and answer the following questions **in English**.

Listen to the recording

(a) Why is the garden mentioned?   **(1 mark)**
(b) What did they use to do before going to bed?   **(1 mark)**

Social media

This page gives you vocabulary about social media to help with listening and reading tasks.

Las redes sociales

Uso las redes sociales para ...
I use social media to ...

intercambiar información personal.
exchange personal information.

compartir fotos y vídeos.
share photos and videoclips.

conocer a gente nueva.   meet new people.

organizar las salidas   arrange to meet
con mis amigos.   up with my friends.

chatear en línea.   chat online.

mandar mensajes a mi novio/a.
send messages to my boyfriend/girlfriend.

escribir blogs.   write blogs.

Para usarlas con seguridad hay que ...
To use it safely you should ...

proteger tu información personal.
protect your personal information.

No hay que ...   You should not ...

compartir las contraseñas.
share your passwords.

abrir mensajes o archivos extraños.
open strange messages or files.

Cognates

☑ Look out for cognates in Spanish. These are words that **resemble**, or are the **same as**, words in English, e.g.
mensaje   message
fotos   photos

☑ Look out for ways to **connect** Spanish words too. This will help you work out the meaning of new words and help you remember vocabulary, e.g.

flor	flower	floristería	florist's
libro	book	librería	bookshop
pan	bread	panadería	bakery
seguro/a	safe	seguridad	safety
un intercambio	an exchange		
intercambiar	to exchange		

Worked example

LISTENING TRACK 5

Listen to Olivia's podcast. What is her opinion about social media? Write the correct letter in the box. **(1 mark)**

A	It is dangerous for adolescents.
B	There should be more safety measures.
C	It is good for sharing photos.

C

Listen to the recording

– En mi opinión, las redes sociales no son peligrosas si vas con cuidado. Las uso porque es fácil compartir fotos con mis amigos.

Listening strategies

Remember to read the statements **before** you begin listening and to predict the types of words or phrases you may hear. While listening and before choosing your answer, think carefully about the **context** of any relevant vocabulary you heard.

The word for 'dangerous' (option A) is mentioned, but in a negative statement: **no son peligrosas si vas con cuidado**. The key to understanding the context and choosing option C is the phrase **es fácil**, which equates to 'is good for ...'.

Now try this

LISTENING TRACK 6

Listen to the whole podcast. What aspect of social media does Olivia like best? Write the correct letter in the box.
(1 mark)

A	You can block users who write offensive remarks.
B	You can communicate with friends in different places.
C	You can arrange dates with friends and classmates.

Listen to the recording

Technology

Technology is part of our everyday life. Make sure you can talk about it in Spanish.

La tecnología

el disco duro

la Xbox / la consola

la pantalla

los altavoces

los videojuegos

la tableta   el móvil   el teclado   el ratón   los auriculares

Usamos la tecnología todos los días

Estamos en contacto con nuestras familias.
We are in touch with our families.
Descargamos MP3/aplicaciones.
We download MP3s/apps.
Subimos / cargamos vídeos.
We upload videoclips.
Mandamos mensajes (de texto).
We send text messages.
Contestamos a los correos electrónicos.
We reply to emails.
Grabamos discos.   We burn disks.
Escribimos a máquina.   We type.

Aiming higher

Use interesting adjectives to describe technology and other topics. Stay clear of over-used adjectives like interesante, divertido or aburrido.

adecuado/a	suitable
breve	brief
flexible	flexible
gratis	free
necesario/a	necessary
nuevo/a	new
numeroso/a	numerous
peligroso/a	dangerous
práctico/a	practical
rápido/a	fast

Worked example

Read the following opinions about technology. Who does not like texting? Write **P** (Pablo), **G** (Gabriela) or **P+G** (Pablo and Gabriela). **(1 mark)**

| P |

Remember that there are a number of ways to express a negative opinion. Pablo does not say **no me gusta** but instead says **es aburrido** to express dislike.

Pablo: Uso el móvil todos los días y siempre descargo canciones nuevas. Creo que es aburrido mandar mensajes de texto. Lo que más me gusta de la tecnología es que la mayoría de las aplicaciones que uso son gratis.

Gabriela: Hay aspectos de los ordenadores que encuentro peligrosos, así que uso mucho el móvil para comunicarme con los amigos. Las tabletas y los ordenadores son buenos para jugar a los videojuegos y por muchos no tienes que pagar. Utilizo la tecnología más para acceder a la información que para hacer los deberes.

Now try this

Read the following opinions about technology. Who expresses which opinion? Write **P** (Pablo), **G** (Gabriela) or **P+G** (Pablo and Gabriela).

(a) Who is concerned about online safety? ☐
(b) Who likes free games? ☐
(c) Who downloads music ☐

(d) Who uses their mobile a lot? ☐
(e) Who uses technology for research? ☐

(5 marks)

9

The internet

There are lots of ways you can use the internet. This page will help you with this specific vocabulary.

Internet

Cuando estoy conectado/a a Internet suelo ...
When I am online I usually ...

hacer compras por Internet	do online shopping
navegar por la red	surf the net
cargar / subir fotos a Instagram	
upload photos to Instagram	
leer páginas web	read webpages
utilizar las salas de chat	use chat rooms
enviar y recibir correos electrónicos	
send and receive emails	
buscar información	look for information
hacer ejercicios interactivos en línea	
do interactive online exercises	

Solía ver vídeos en YouTube.
I used to watch videos on YouTube.

Talking about what usually happens

You use the verb soler + the infinitive to talk about what someone **usually** does.

suelo	I usually ...
sueles	you usually (singular / informal) ...
suele	he / she / you (sing. polite) usually ...
solemos	we usually ...
soléis	you usually (plural / informal) ...
suelen	they / you (pl. polite) usually ...

Suelo descargar música.
I usually download music.

Knowing the **imperfect** form can help you improve your performance in listening tests.

Worked example

Translate the following passage into **Spanish**.   (12 marks)

> My friends and I use the internet nearly every day. At school we sometimes need to look for information or do online exercises in Spanish classes. Last week I made a webpage and it was quite easy. Later I am going to upload photos of my party.

Mis amigos y yo utilizamos Internet casi todos los días. En el instituto a veces tenemos que buscar información o hacer ejercicios en línea durante las clases de español. La semana pasada hice una página web y fue bastante fácil. Más tarde voy a subir fotos de mi fiesta.

Aiming higher

For the translation task, be prepared to write sentences using verb forms that express present, past and future events. It is therefore really important to learn your verb endings carefully.

Remember that 'the internet' never uses an article and always takes a capital letter in Spanish: Utilizamos Internet casi todos los días.

Now try this

Translate the following passage into **Spanish**.   (12 marks)

> Normally I do online shopping as it is cheap and quite easy. At home my parents usually send and receive emails but my sister and I read webpages and use chatrooms. Last year I bought a new mobile phone online and it was not difficult. Tomorrow I am going to surf the net to look for some video games.

Pros and cons of technology

Use these phrases to prepare your own opinions on using technology.

La tecnología: las ventajas y las desventajas

🙂

permitir más comunicación e interacción
to allow more communication and interaction
hablar con la familia en el extranjero
to talk with family abroad
comprar y vender por Internet
to buy and sell online
jugar a los videojuegos con amigos
to play video games with friends
leer las noticias   **to read the news**

🙁

el peligro de   **the danger of**
conocer a extraños con malas intenciones
meeting strangers with bad intentions
ver contenido inapropiado y nocivo
watching inappropriate and harmful content
el acoso en las redes sociales
bullying on social networking sites
acceso a los datos personales
access to personal data

Using ser in different tenses

Recognising ser (to be) in the past, present and future is key for higher-level reading questions.

Present	Imperfect	Future
soy	era	seré
eres	eras	serás
es	era	será

El problema más grave es si alguien accede a tu cuenta bancaria.
The worst problem is if someone accesses your bank account.

Escuchar y ver música por Internet es guay.
Listening to and watching music online is cool.

Worked example

1 Read this article about the internet.

> Existen muchos problemas con Internet. Antes, el problema más grave era el acoso en las redes sociales, pero los expertos dicen que actualmente el problema más serio es el fraude en las cuentas bancarias. También dicen que dentro de diez años el contenido nocivo será el problema más grave.

Which is the correct sentence? Write the correct letter in the box.

A	There are lots of problems with the internet.
B	Online bullying is the most serious problem.

[A]   **(1 mark)**

- Knowing **ser** in the present, imperfect and future will enable you to distinguish between the problems.
- Time phrases – **antes** (before), **actualmente** (currently) and **dentro de diez años** (within ten years) – can also help distinguish time frames.

Now try this

What statements does the article in the worked example make?

A	Social networking sites are always safe.
B	Fraud is now a bigger problem than online bullying.
C	Bank accounts are at risk from fraud.

D	In ten years, experts will solve the fraud issue.
E	Fraud will always be the main problem.
F	Websites with harmful content will become more of a problem.

Write the correct letters in the boxes.   ☐ ☐ ☐

(3 marks)

Hobbies

Prepare to talk and write about hobbies using this page. Research any hobbies you do that aren't covered here so that you can talk about them easily.

El ocio

Juego a los videojuegos.	I play video games.
Toco la batería.	I play the drums.
Hago piragüismo.	I do canoeing.
Voy en monopatín.	I skateboard.
Bailo.	I dance.
Voy / Salgo a caminar.	I go for walks.
Salgo con amigos.	I go out with friends.

Veo muchas series de televisión.
I watch lots of television series.

Mi pasatiempo preferido es el patinaje en línea.
My favourite hobby is rollerblading.

Escucha música.
She listens to music.

Present tense (regular verbs)

To form the present tense of regular verbs, replace the infinitive ending as follows:

> Grammar page 88

	hablar – to speak	comer – to eat	vivir – to live
I	hablo	como	vivo
you	hablas	comes	vives
he / she / it	habla	come	vive
we	hablamos	comemos	vivimos
you	habláis	coméis	vivís
they	hablan	comen	viven

Some verbs have an irregular form in the present tense for the first person singular (yo).
hacer ➡ hago
salir ➡ salgo
ver ➡ veo
For more information on irregular verbs, go to page 90.

Worked example

LISTENING TRACK 7

Listen to the recording. What does Javier like doing? Write the correct letter in the box.

A	going swimming
B	skateboarding
C	watching TV

☐ B   **(1 mark)**

Listen to the recording

– ¿Qué te gusta hacer, Javier?
– Me encanta ir en monopatín. ¡Es fantástico!

Listening strategies

Learning vocabulary is key to completing listening tasks successfully. For each topic, make lists of words that you find difficult to remember and ask someone to test you on them.

Listen out for key nouns and verbs to help you answer. You cannot just rely on your knowledge of cognates. Here you need to know **patinaje** and **natación** as well as **música** and **televisión**.

Now try this

LISTENING TRACK 8

Listen to the whole recording from the worked example. What does each person like doing? Write the correct letter in each box.

A	reading
B	shopping
C	watching films
D	swimming
E	listening to music
F	playing video games

Carmen ☐

Teresa ☐

Leonardo ☐

Listen to the recording

(3 marks)

Music

Make sure you are able to give your opinion about music and music events.

La música

Estoy aprendiendo a tocar ...
I am learning to play ...

el piano   la trompeta   el violín   la flauta dulce

la batería   la flauta   el saxofón   el clarinete

Fui a un concierto de música clásica.
I went to a classical music concert.
Escuché música rap.   I listened to rap music.
Fui al festival de música pop.
I went to the pop festival.
Tocaron muchas canciones famosas.
They played lots of famous songs.
Me encanta la música folklórica.
I love folk music.

Describing events: preterite vs imperfect

To describe a music event, you use the **preterite** tense when you talk about **single/completed** events in the past.

Participamos en un espectáculo.
We took part in a show.

Anoche escuché a mi grupo favorito.
I listened to my favourite band last night.

Tocó la guitarra.
She played the guitar.

However, you use the **imperfect** tense when you describe **background** details.

Había un ambiente especial.
There was a special atmosphere.

El teatro era antiguo y grande.
The theatre was old and big.

Worked example

SPEAKING

Answer the question as fully as possible.
• ¿Te gusta la música?

Sí, me gusta mucho y estoy aprendiendo a tocar el violín en la orquesta del instituto. Ayer un amigo mío y yo fuimos a un concierto de música clásica. Fue increíble.

AIMING HIGHER

Para mí, la música es muy importante ya que nos puede dar mucho placer. Antes tocaba la flauta dulce pero ahora toco la trompeta. La música es importantísima en muchas celebraciones como bodas o fiestas de cumpleaños.
El mes pasado fui a un espectáculo de música y baile tradicionales en el pueblo donde vivo. El ambiente era estupendo y a todo el mundo le gustó escuchar tantas melodías fantásticas.

Using both present and past tenses – me gusta, fuimos – creates variety. Including a present continuous phrase – estoy aprendiendo a tocar – also helps to raise the language level.

Extending the response with further information (about why music is important) improves the content and uses more complex opinion language. This answer also employs a good range of tenses: present, preterite and imperfect.
Using the superlative makes an ordinary adjective more interesting – importantísimo.

Now try this

SPEAKING TRACK 9

Now you answer the same question.
• ¿Te gusta la música?

Try this yourself and then listen to the sample response to get some more ideas.

Listen to the recording

Music events

Be prepared to talk about concerts and music events.

Los eventos musicales

Mis amigos y yo fuimos a un concierto.
My friends and I went to a concert.
Estuve tres horas en el concierto.
I spent three hours at the concert.
Bailamos mucho.   We danced a lot.
El grupo cantó todas mis canciones preferidas.
The band sang all my favourite songs.
Mi amigo me compró una camiseta.
My friend bought me a T-shirt.
Saqué muchas fotos.   I took lots of photos.
Mis amigos comieron hamburguesas y bebieron limonada.
My friends ate burgers and drank lemonade.
El espectáculo fue impresionante.
The show was impressive.
Lo pasamos bomba.   We had a great time.
El escenario era muy grande. The stage was really big.
Había más de 20.000 espectadores.
There were more than 20,000 spectators.
El ambiente estaba animado.   The atmosphere was lively.

Expressing opinions about past events

Use the **preterite** tense to give your opinion about an event that has already taken place.
El concierto fue estupendo.
The concert was great.
Me divertí mucho.
I enjoyed myself a lot.
Lo pasé muy bien.
I had a really good time.
Me gustó escuchar mis canciones favoritas.
I liked listening to my favourite songs.
Fuimos a un concierto de rock y fue sensacional.
We went to a rock concert and it was sensational.

Worked example

SPEAKING

Look at the photo and prepare your answer.

- ¿Te gustaría ir a un festival de dos o tres días?

Sí, me encantaría ir. Creo que el ambiente sería fantástico. El problema es si hace mal tiempo y llueve todo el tiempo. ¡Sería muy incómodo!

Exam alert

In your speaking tasks:
- Respond to each question as fully as you can.
- If you need to hear a question again, you can ask the examiner to repeat it.
- Do use the preparation time to think about your answers, but don't read out whole sentences that you've prepared in advance.

Now try this

SPEAKING
TRACK 10

Listen to the recording

Now prepare your own answers to all the questions below. Then listen to the recording and answer in the pauses.

1   ¿Qué hay en la foto?
2   ¿Te gustan los conciertos de música? ¿Por qué (no)?
3   ¿Cómo fue el último concierto que viste?
4   ¿Te gustaría ir a un festival de dos o tres días?
5   ¿Quién es tu cantante favorito? ¿Por qué?

Sport

When you write about sport, remember to use the appropriate verb – jugar, practicar or hacer.

Los deportes

¿Qué deporte practicas?	What sport do you do?
Juego …	I play …
al fútbol.	
al baloncesto.	
al tenis.	
Practico …	I do …
el ciclismo.	
el jogging / footing.	
la equitación.	
la gimnasia.	
Hago …	I do …
patinaje.	

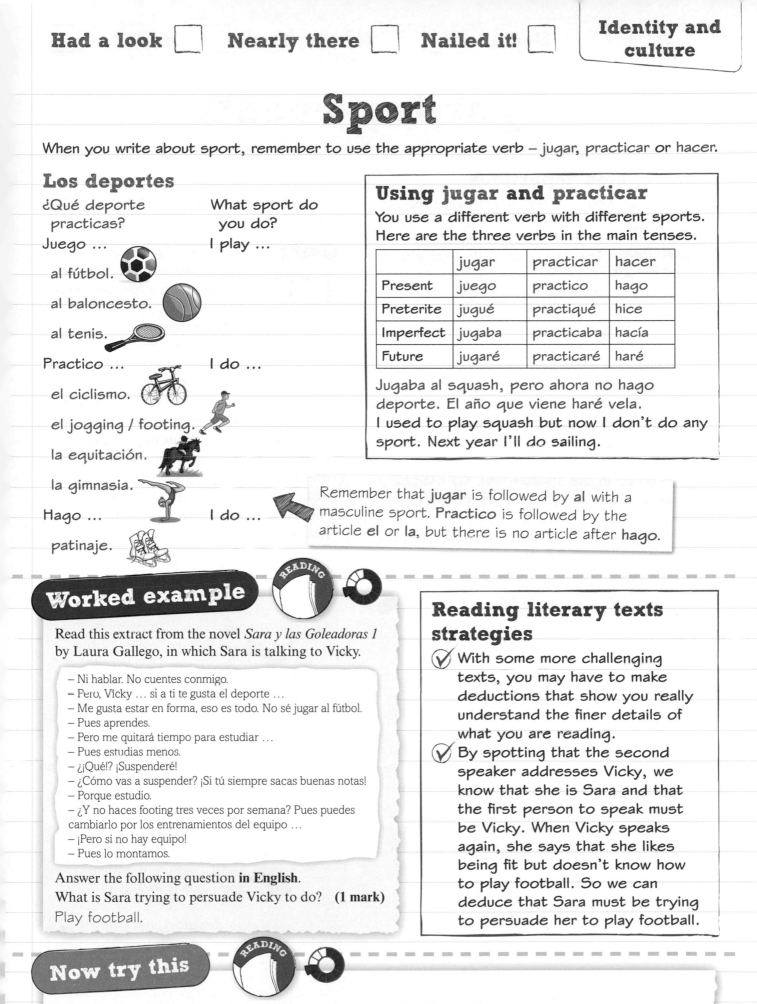

Using jugar and practicar

You use a different verb with different sports. Here are the three verbs in the main tenses.

	jugar	practicar	hacer
Present	juego	practico	hago
Preterite	jugué	practiqué	hice
Imperfect	jugaba	practicaba	hacía
Future	jugaré	practicaré	haré

Jugaba al squash, pero ahora no hago deporte. El año que viene haré vela.
I used to play squash but now I don't do any sport. Next year I'll do sailing.

> Remember that **jugar** is followed by **al** with a masculine sport. **Practico** is followed by the article **el** or **la**, but there is no article after **hago**.

Worked example

READING

Read this extract from the novel *Sara y las Goleadoras 1* by Laura Gallego, in which Sara is talking to Vicky.

– Ni hablar. No cuentes conmigo.
– Pero, Vicky … si a ti te gusta el deporte …
– Me gusta estar en forma, eso es todo. No sé jugar al fútbol.
– Pues aprendes.
– Pero me quitará tiempo para estudiar …
– Pues estudias menos.
– ¿¡Qué!? ¡Suspenderé!
– ¿Cómo vas a suspender? ¡Si tú siempre sacas buenas notas!
– Porque estudio.
– ¿Y no haces footing tres veces por semana? Pues puedes cambiarlo por los entrenamientos del equipo …
– ¡Pero si no hay equipo!
– Pues lo montamos.

Answer the following question **in English.**
What is Sara trying to persuade Vicky to do? **(1 mark)**
Play football.

Reading literary texts strategies

☑ With some more challenging texts, you may have to make deductions that show you really understand the finer details of what you are reading.

☑ By spotting that the second speaker addresses Vicky, we know that she is Sara and that the first person to speak must be Vicky. When Vicky speaks again, she says that she likes being fit but doesn't know how to play football. So we can deduce that Sara must be trying to persuade her to play football.

Now try this

READING

Read the extract again. Answer the following questions **in English.**
(a) Apart from Vicky's lack of experience, what other reason does she give for not getting involved? **(1 mark)**
(b) Why is Vicky unlikely to follow Sara's suggestion about schoolwork? **(1 mark)**
(c) What does Sara say about Vicky's school achievements? **(1 mark)**
(d) What is Sara's final time-saving suggestion to Vicky? **(1 mark)**

Sporting events

You need to understand and use language related to sporting events.

Los eventos deportivos

Las ventajas son ...   The advantages are ...

Hay un ambiente especial.
There is a special atmosphere.

El evento que más me interesa es ...
The event that interests me most is ...
Ver un partido en directo es emocionante.
Watching a live match is exciting.
Es entretenido estar con los otros aficionados.
It's entertaining to be with the other fans.
Es una actividad que hacemos en familia.
It's an activity we do as a family.
Es divertido estar en el estadio con mis amigos.
It's fun to be in the stadium with my friends.
Me gusta hablar del partido después con mi padre.
I like to talk about the match afterwards with my dad.

Las desventajas son ...
The disadvantages are ...

A veces algunos aficionados se comportan violentamente.
Sometimes a few fans behave violently.
Las entradas cuestan mucho dinero.
The tickets cost a lot of money.
Cuando hay un partido en la ciudad, siempre hay mucho tráfico.
When there is a match in town, there is always a lot of traffic.
No me interesa mucho el deporte.
I'm not really interested in sport.
Prefiero ver el deporte en la tele.
I prefer to watch sport on the TV.
Mi novio está obsesionado con el fútbol.
My boyfriend is obsessed with football.

Worked example

WRITING

Escribe un artículo sobre los eventos deportivos en tu ciudad. Menciona:
• lo que piensas de los eventos
• la última vez que fuiste a un evento deportivo   **(32 marks)**

> En mi ciudad hay partidos de fútbol y de rugby todos los fines de semana. Son muy populares y miles de personas asisten cada semana. Yo voy a ver a mi equipo favorito con mi padre todos los sábados y es muy emocionante estar en el estadio porque hay un ambiente fenomenal. En mi opinión, los eventos deportivos son excelentes porque unen a la gente e inspiran a los jóvenes.

AIMING HIGHER

> El sábado pasado fue muy especial para mí porque mi equipo jugó un partido importante de la Copa. Mi padre y yo viajamos a Londres para verlo y pasamos la mañana visitando sitios de interés en la capital. Llegamos al estadio media hora antes del partido y lo pasamos bomba comiendo perritos calientes y cantando con los otros aficionados. Desafortunadamente, perdimos cero a uno pero fue una experiencia inolvidable.

Make sure you recognise that these prompts are asking for an opinion, and remember to justify the opinion by giving reasons.

Giving interesting reasons and justifications such as **unen a la gente** and **inspiran a los jóvenes** makes this candidate's language more sophisticated.

Mentioning a negative point, and introducing it with a suitable connective such as **desafortunadamente**, gives variety to this account and shows competence in expressing ideas.

Now try this

WRITING

Write your own article, including the information requested in the bullet points in the worked example.
Write at least **150** words **in Spanish**.
(32 marks)

Films

Make sure you are able to talk about films and buy tickets at a cinema.

El cine

una comedia	a comedy
una película romántica	a romantic film
una película de dibujos animados / de animación	a cartoon / an animated film
una película de ciencia ficción	a science fiction film
una película de aventuras	an adventure film
una película de suspense	a thriller
una película de terror / de miedo	a horror film
una película de artes marciales	a martial arts film

¿Quieres ir al cine el domingo?
Do you want to go to the cinema on Sunday?

No puedo, estoy ocupado/a.
I can't, I'm busy.

Me encantaría ir.   I would love to go.

Voy a sacar las entradas por Internet.
I am going to buy tickets online.

¿Dónde quedamos?
Where shall we meet?

Podemos quedar en la estación.
We can meet at the station.

Days of the week

lunes	Monday
martes	Tuesday
miércoles	Wednesday
jueves	Thursday
viernes	Friday
sábado	Saturday
domingo	Sunday

To specify a day you regularly do something, use los:
Los sábados vemos películas.
On Saturdays we watch films.

To specify a particular day, use el:
Quedamos el lunes a las cinco de la tarde.
Let's meet on Monday at 5pm.

por la tarde / noche	in the afternoon / at night
los fines de semana	at weekends
todos los días	every day

Worked example

LISTENING TRACK 11

Isabel is talking about films.
What type of film does she prefer?

Listen to the recording

week adventure fun martial arts
Saturday exciting interesting month

<u>adventure</u> .   **(1 mark)**

– Me chiflan las películas de artes marciales, pero no son mis favoritas. En realidad, prefiero las películas de aventuras.

Exam alert

Make sure you **don't rush** to complete the task, or you could miss important details. Listen **carefully**, right to the end of the recording, before you make your final decision.

The key to choosing the correct answer is to identify which films she prefers rather than films she likes. She says **prefiero** for adventure films and uses **me chiflan** for martial arts films.

Now try this

LISTENING TRACK 12

Listen to the recording

Listen to the rest of the recording from the worked example and answer the questions **in English**.

(a) Why does she like adventure films?   **(1 mark)**

(b) When is she going to watch a film at home?   **(1 mark)**

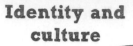
TV

You need to be able to describe the **types** of programmes you watch, as well as naming them.

Los programas de televisión

los programas de deportes	sports programmes
el telediario / las noticias	the news
los documentales	documentaries
los concursos	gameshows
las series policíacas	crime series
los dibujos animados	cartoons
las telenovelas	soaps
un programa de telerrealidad	a reality TV programme

Note that you always use the definite article (the) for the items you compare.

Aiming higher

You need to give or understand **reasons** for your likes and dislikes. Use comparatives to impress!

The comparative

Grammar page 85

The comparative is used to compare two things. It is formed as follows:

más + adjective + que = more ... than
menos + adjective + que = less ... than

The adjective agrees with the noun it describes:

Las telenovelas son menos aburridas que los concursos.
Soap operas are less boring than gameshows.

Los dibujos animados son más interesantes que los programas de telerrealidad.
Cartoons are more interesting than reality TV programmes.

Worked example

Read this advertisement for a television channel.

Canal Concurso es un canal nuevo que empezó en México hace tres meses. Ofrece una programación animada sin ser infantil. Se pueden ver una gran variedad de concursos para todas las edades. Actualmente nuestro concurso más popular es de Japón, con subtítulos en español, y los participantes son niños de ocho a trece años. Hay que verlo. ¡Es sorprendente!

Answer the question **in English**.
How long has the channel been broadcasting for?

(1 mark)

3 months

Aiming higher

Look at **Spanish websites** about films and TV programmes. Not only will you practise your vocabulary, you'll also develop good reading strategies that will help you in the exam, such as:
- ✓ using what you know to rule out some options
- ✓ recognising cognates
- ✓ using grammar structures to help work out unknown words.

 Now try this

Read the text from the worked example again and answer the questions **in English**.

(a) How does the advertisement describe the programmes the channel shows? **(1 mark)**

(b) Who are the gameshows on the channel for? **(1 mark)**

(c) Where is the most popular show from? **(1 mark)**

(d) Who can go on this show? **(1 mark)**

Food and drink

Make sure you revise food and drink words carefully, as there are not many cognates to help you!

Ir de tapas

Me gusta ir de tapas.	I like to go out for tapas.
la carne fría cortada en lonchas	cold sliced meat
la tortilla de patatas	potato omelette
las albóndigas	meatballs
el pincho moruno / la brocheta	shish kebab / meat on skewers
el queso (de cabra)	(goat's) cheese
el pescado	fish
el arroz	rice
la ensalada mixta	mixed salad
los pimientos cocidos	roasted peppers
el marisco	seafood
los panecillos	bread rolls
la cerveza	el zumo de fruta
el agua mineral	el vino
el refresco	

Articles: 'the', 'a' and 'some'

There are four different ways to say 'the' in Spanish.

Grammar page 82

	Singular	Plural
Masculine	el atún	los espaguetis
Feminine	la sopa	las salchichas

There are two ways to say 'a', plus two plural forms, which mean 'some'.

	Singular	Plural
Masculine	un bocadillo a sandwich	unos bocadillos some sandwiches
Feminine	una loncha a slice	unas lonchas some slices

Worked example

You are in a restaurant in Spain. The teacher will play the part of the waiter/waitress and will speak first.

Usted está en un restaurante de España.

1 Bebida – descripción
¿En qué puedo servirle?
Me gustaría tomar un zumo de fruta.

2 Comida española – razón
Muy bien. ¿Le gusta la comida española?
Me encanta la comida española porque es muy variada y deliciosa.

3 !
Sí, claro. Habla muy bien el español. ¿De dónde es?
Gracias. Soy inglesa.

4 Planes – hoy
¿Qué planes tiene para hoy?
Voy a hacer una excursión en bici.
Muy bien.

5 ? Menú del día
¿Hay menú del día?
Claro que sí.

Exam alert

In the role play section of the speaking exam, make sure you pay attention to the register you must use – tú or usted. Remember to use the correct verb endings when asking questions.

Exam alert

For the Foundation tier, you will need to ask a question, shown by ?. In the Higher tier role play, there are **two** questions for you to ask. Both Foundation and Higher role plays include a response to something you have not prepared, shown by !. Here the unexpected question is ¿De dónde es? and the candidate answers by giving his/her nationality.

Be prepared in a role play to answer questions or give opinions on a range of topics. For example, here the role play is set in a restaurant but you also have to say your nationality and give your opinion about Spanish food.

The unexpected question is **¿Y para beber?** Can you think of any other questions you could have been asked here?

Now try this

Listen to the recording

Prepare your own answers to the following restaurant role play prompts. Then listen to the audio recording of the teacher's part and fill in your answers in the pauses.

1 Mesa – número de personas
2 Comida – descripción
3 !
4 Comida – opinión
5 ? Comida - precio

Eating in a café

Make sure you revise lots of café vocabulary for understanding texts and role play situations.

Comer en una cafetería

¿Qué va a tomar? — What would you like?

Voy a tomar ... — I'll have ...

agua (mineral) con gas. — sparkling (mineral) water.

un café (solo). — a (black) coffee.

una limonada. — a lemonade.

un té. — a tea.

un zumo de naranja. — an orange juice.

con azúcar — with sugar

con leche — with milk

con / sin hielo — with / without ice

un bocadillo — a sandwich

una hamburguesa — a hamburger

un helado — an ice cream

un perrito caliente — a hot dog

un vaso — a glass

una botella — a bottle

una taza — a cup

High frequency words

Watch out for key but easily overlooked words that affect meaning.

café con azúcar — coffee with sugar

café sin azúcar — coffee without sugar

nunca — never

siempre — always

solo — only

hasta — until

todo el mundo — everybody

salvo / excepto — except

a causa de — because of

En mi familia todo el mundo bebe té sin leche.

In my family everyone drinks tea without milk.

Siempre meriendo galletas.

I always snack on biscuits in the afternoon.

Worked example

Read the texts about going to cafés.

> **Andrés:** Suelo ir a una cafetería cada mañana sobre las once. Voy con mis compañeros de trabajo durante el descanso. A veces tomo un poco de pan con tomate si tengo hambre. Muchas veces compro una botella de agua también porque el café puede ser muy fuerte. Siempre hay que mirar el reloj para no volver tarde al trabajo.
>
> **Begoña:** Me reúno cada sábado por la tarde con un grupo de amigos. Nos vemos en la cafetería y tomamos café. Siempre probamos alguno de los excelentes pasteles que venden allí – son riquísimos. Charlamos y hacemos planes y a veces estamos allí casi dos horas. Es muy agradable sentarse en la terraza y ver pasar a la gente.

Match the statement to the correct person.

Write **A** (Andrés), **B** (Begoña) or **A+B** (Andrés and Begoña).

Who goes to a café only at weekends? [B] **(1 mark)**

To help you choose the correct answer for this type of exercise, you must read both texts thoroughly. Think about the words you will need to look out for. For example: weekend ➡ **fin de semana** or **sábado** or **domingo**; afternoon ➡ **a las tres** or **después de comer** or **tarde**.

Now try this

Read the text in the worked example and match each statement to the correct person. Write **A** (Andrés), **B** (Begoña) or **A+B** (Andrés and Begoña).

(a) Who often has something to eat in the café? [ ]

(b) Who goes to the café in the afternoon? [ ]

(c) Who sits back and relaxes in the café? [ ]

(d) Who goes with colleagues? [ ]

(e) Who drinks coffee? [ ]

(5 marks)

Eating in a restaurant

Use this vocabulary to talk about eating out in restaurants.

Comer en un restaurante

la carta	menu
el plato del día	dish of the day
el menú del día	menu of the day/ fixed price menu
el primer plato	starter
el secundo plato	main course
el postre	dessert
la cuenta	bill
el autoservicio	self service
el aperitivo	a drink (or food) before your meal

¿Quiere pan y mantequilla?
Would you like bread and butter?

Quiero ...	I want ...
el bistec con patatas fritas.	steak and chips.
el cordero con guisantes.	lamb with peas.
¡Buen provecho! / ¡Que aproveche!	Enjoy your meal!

Using beber and comer in the preterite

	beber – to drink	comer – to eat
I	bebí	comí
he / she / it	bebió	comió
we	bebimos	comimos
they	bebieron	comieron

Para celebrar la Pascua comimos arroz con leche en un restaurante. To celebrate Easter, we ate rice pudding in a restaurant.

Worked example

Read this extract from *Una Madre* by Alejandro Palomas about a disappointing trip to a restaurant.

> La verdad es que la elección del restaurante no pudo ser menos apropiada. A Silvia se le ocurrió que la mejor opción para la ocasión era el *Asador de las dos Castillas*, "un sitio estupendo donde se come de maravilla. Además, tiene un par de reservados (mesas) donde se está muy tranquilo. Yo me encargo de llamar. A los chicos de la oficina les encanta", dijo, no dando mucha opción a que nadie propusiera alguna alternativa. "Luego, si terminamos temprano, podríamos ir a alguna terraza a tomar el café", concedió.
>
> El sitio tenía poco de estupendo, aunque sí resultó ser tranquilo, básicamente porque no había ni un *alma. El comedor olía a desinfectante de lavabos ...
>
> *alma = soul

Answer the following question **in English.**
What does the author say could not have been less appropriate? **(1 mark)**
The choice of restaurant

Reading literary texts

☑ Don't expect to be able to translate everything in the text. You won't need to understand everything in order to answer the questions.

☑ Be prepared to scan the text to look for the answers. In the example, the phrase 'less appropriate' leads you to the first sentence of the text and the words just before *menos apropiada* give you the answer.

Now try this

Read the extract in the worked example again. Answer the following questions **in English.**

(a) What **two** reasons does Silvia give for choosing the *Asador*? **(2 marks)**

(b) Who also recommended it? **(1 mark)**

(c) What does she suggest for after the meal? **(1 mark)**

(d) Was the restaurant busy? Give a reason for your answer. **(1 mark)**

(e) What was the problem with the dining area? **(1 mark)**

21

Meals at home

Eating at home is an important topic. This page will help you talk and write about it.

Las comidas en casa

el desayuno	breakfast
el almuerzo / la comida	lunch
la merienda	afternoon snack
la cena	dinner
Es importante ...	It's important ...
comer juntos.	to eat together.
sentarse a la mesa.	to sit down at the table.
compartir experiencias.	to share experiences.

Desayunamos cereales y fruta.
We have cereal and fruit for breakfast.

Nos gusta comer pollo asado.
We like to eat roast chicken.

Las chuletas de cerdo son deliciosas.
Pork chops are delicious.

la carne picada	mince
los espaguetis	spaghetti
las verduras	vegetables
los huevos fritos	fried eggs
el filete muy hecho	steak well done

To say how long you have been doing something

Use desde hace + present tense **or** llevo + the gerund:

> Grammar page 92

Como alimentos ecológicos desde hace dos años.
I have been eating organic food for two years.

Llevo cinco meses comiendo pescado fresco.
I have been eating fresh fish for five months.

To say you have just done something

Use acabo de + infinitive:
Acabo de volver de Italia.
I have just returned from Italy.

Worked example

Read the article below.

Las comidas en casa

Hoy en día parece que nadie tiene tiempo para nada, todos corremos de un sitio a otro, de un momento a otro. Desde hace unos años las familias tienen cada vez menos tiempo de sentarse a la mesa para comer juntos. De hecho, la comida sabe mejor porque se comparte el momento y las anécdotas familiares. Comer juntos también ayuda a la comunicación entre padres e hijos. A veces es difícil lograrlo, para ello se necesita organización. Acabo de cenar con mis vecinos y en su casa los niños aprenden a interesarse por el resto de la familia.

Answer the following question **in English**.
What has decreased in the last few years? **(1 mark)**
time spent eating together as a family

Remember that you do not need to answer in full sentences.

Learning vocabulary

To prepare for your exam, you need to learn lots of vocabulary.
- ☑ **Look** at the words and memorise them.
- ☑ **Cover** the words.
- ☑ **Write** the words.
- ☑ **Look** again.
- ☑ **See** how many you got right.

Start by covering the English words. When you're confident, cover the Spanish words and see if you can remember them from the English prompts.

Now try this

Read the article in the worked example again. Answer the following questions **in English**.
(a) What effect does eating together have on food? **(1 mark)**
(b) How can you overcome difficulties over eating together? **(1 mark)**
(c) What do children learn from eating with adults? **(1 mark)**

Shopping for food

Not many fruits and vegetables have similar names in Spanish, so learn them carefully.

¿Qué desea?

Deme ... , por favor.	Give me ... please.
¿Algo más?	Anything else?
Nada más.	Nothing else.
un melocotón	a peach
un plátano	a banana
unas frambuesas	raspberries
un albaricoque	an apricot
una ciruela	a plum
unas uvas	grapes
un pomelo	a grapefruit
una naranja	an orange
un pepino	a cucumber
una coliflor	a cauliflower
unas judías / alubias	beans
una lechuga	a lettuce

Quantities

In Spanish you use de (of) with quantities, even with grams and kilograms:

una lata de tomates	a tin of tomatoes
una barra de pan	a loaf of bread
una caja de galletas	a box of biscuits
una botella de agua	a bottle of water
un tarro de mermelada	a jar of marmalade
un paquete de caramelos	a bag of sweets
doscientos cincuenta gramos de ...	250 grams of ...
quinientos gramos de ...	500 grams of ...
medio kilo de ...	half a kilo of ...
un kilo de ...	1 kilo of ...
una docena de huevos	a dozen eggs

unas cerezas   una manzana   unas fresas   unas zanahorias

una piña   una cebolla   unos guisantes

To say 'a slice of ... ', you use **una loncha de queso** for 'a slice of cheese', but **una rebanada de pan** for 'a slice of bread'.

Worked example

LISTENING TRACK 14

Listen to the conversation in the shop. Complete the sentence. Write the correct letter in the box.

The customer would like 500g of ...

A	cherries
B	strawberries
C	raspberries

B   **(1 mark)**

– Hola, buenos días. ¿Qué desea?
– Deme quinientos gramos de fresas y ochocientos gramos de cerezas, por favor.

Listen to the recording

Exam alert

If you are not sure, have a guess to give you a chance of gaining a mark. As well as learning fruits and vegetables, make sure you learn quantities and revise your numbers!

Now try this

LISTENING TRACK 15

Listen to the recording

Listen to the rest of the conversation. Complete the sentences. Write the correct letter in each box.

(a) The shopkeeper recommends the ...   A strawberries   B pears   C apples   ☐ **(1 mark)**
(b) The shopkeeper has run out of ...   A plums   B grapes   C eggs   ☐ **(1 mark)**
(c) The cost of the food purchased is ...   A 4,50€   B 5,00€   C 14,50€   ☐ **(1 mark)**

23

Opinions about food

Make sure you can give and understand opinions about food.

Opiniones sobre la comida

¿Qué tipo de comida te gusta?	What kind of food do you like?
Mi comida favorita es ...	My favourite food is ...
la comida española	Spanish food
la comida griega	Greek food
la comida india	Indian food
la comida italiana	Italian food
porque es ...	because it's ...
delicioso/a	delicious
malo/a para la salud	unhealthy
nutritivo/a	nutritious
picante	spicy
rico/a	tasty
sabroso/a	tasty
salado/a	salty
sano/a	healthy

Using -ísimo for emphasis

Add -ísimo to the end of an adjective to make it stronger.

buenísimo/a   really good
riquísimo/a   really tasty

Expressing a range of opinions

Creo que ...	I think that ...
♥ Me gusta ...	I like ...
No me gusta (nada) ...	I don't like ... (at all)
Odio ...	I hate ...
En mi opinión ...	In my opinion ...

Creo que la comida española es buenísima.
I think Spanish food is really nice.
Odio las anchoas porque son saladísimas.
I hate anchovies because they are salty.

Don't forget to make adjectives agree!

Worked example

Listen to the recording. What type of food does María cook? Write the correct letter in the box. **(1 mark)**

A	Spanish
B	English
C	Indian

A

– ¡Hola! Me llamo María. Soy cocinera y trabajo en un restaurante español de Londres.

Listening strategies

☑ Be patient and continue to listen **carefully** even if the answers don't come up in the first few sentences.

☑ Remember that people don't always describe things directly. Listen out for **comparatives** and use these to work out opinions which aren't stated directly.

Now try this

Listen to the whole recording from the worked example and answer the following questions **in English**.

(a) According to María, which food is healthier than Indian food? **(1 mark)**

(b) What nationality is María's boyfriend? **(1 mark)**

(c) She is busy, but why else is it good that he cooks meals for her? **(1 mark)**

Celebrations

Be prepared to talk about how you and your family celebrate.

¡Felicidades!

la fiesta de cumpleaños	birthday party
la boda	wedding
el aniversario	anniversary
la Nochebuena	Christmas Eve
la Nochevieja	New Year's Eve
Papá Noel	Father Christmas
el Día de Reyes	Epiphany (6th January)
la Semana Santa	Easter

¡Feliz Navidad!
Happy Christmas

¡Felices Pascuas!
Happy Easter

¡Feliz cumpleaños!
Happy birthday

¡Feliz Año Nuevo!
Happy New Year

Using different tenses

Present

Normalmente, celebramos ...
Normally, we celebrate ...
Vienen nuestros abuelos / primos.
Our grandparents / cousins come.

Preterite

Invité a ...	I invited ...
Comimos ...	We ate ...
¡Fue (genial)!	It was (great)!

Imperfect

Antes íbamos a ...	We used to go to ...
Había mucha gente.	There were a lot of people.

Future

Iremos a ...	We will go to ...
Será (fantástico).	It will be (fantastic).

Worked example

Escribe un blog sobre las celebraciones.

> Normalmente, para celebrar mi cumpleaños voy al cine. Cumplí quince años el fin de semana pasado. Por la tarde fui al cine con mis mejores amigos y por la noche celebramos una fiesta en casa. Invité a diez amigos y mis primos vinieron también. Lo pasé fenomenal.

Here the preterite tense has been used successfully (**cumplí, fui, invité, vinieron,** etc.). The student has also included an opinion (**lo pasé fenomenal**).

AIMING HIGHER

> Siempre celebramos mi cumpleaños, la Semana Santa, la Navidad y la Nochevieja en casa con toda la familia. La Navidad me parece el día más emocionante del año porque siempre lo celebramos con mucha comida, y varios regalos. Hace dos años estuvimos en España y me encantó ver cómo se celebra el Día de Reyes pero este año nos quedaremos en casa.

This has a greater variety of vocabulary and present, preterite and future tenses (**celebramos, estuvimos, nos quedaremos**). Interesting and complex structures also raise the level of the description (**la Navidad me parece ... , me encantó ver cómo se celebra ...**).

Now try this

Escribe un blog sobre tus celebraciones en casa. Menciona:
* qué haces normalmente para tu cumpleaños
* qué hiciste la Navidad pasada
* por qué son importantes las celebraciones
* los planes que tienes para una celebración en el futuro.

Escribe aproximadamente **90** palabras **en español**.

(16 marks)

Customs

Make sure you can understand different types of texts about Spanish culture.

Las costumbres españolas

España es un país de costumbres.
Spain is a country with lots of customs.

Los españoles suelen … Spanish people tend to …

ir de tapas / tapear. — go out to eat tapas.

echar(se) una siesta. — take a nap (traditionally after lunch).

salir a tomar algo en las terrazas. — go out to cafés with terraces.

pasear. — go for a stroll.

comer las doce uvas en Nochevieja. — eat the twelve grapes for New Year's Eve (one on each stroke of midnight).

saludar a la gente con dos besos. — greet people with two kisses.

ir a una corrida de toros. — go to a bull fight.

comer más tarde que otros europeos. — eat later than other Europeans.

Muchos españoles se acuestan tarde. — Many Spanish people go to bed late.

Los horarios de las tiendas son más amplios que en otros países. — Shop opening hours are longer than in other countries.

Special calendar dates

Learn these special days in Spanish.

la Nochebuena	Christmas Eve
la Navidad	Christmas
la Cuaresma	Lent
la Pascua / la Semana Santa	Easter / Holy Week
el Viernes Santo	Good Friday
el Lunes de Pascua	Easter Monday
¡Feliz cumpleaños!	Happy birthday!
¡Feliz Año Nuevo!	Happy New Year!

¡Feliz Navidad!
Happy Christmas!

The seasons

el otoño	autumn
la primavera	spring
el verano	summer
el invierno	winter

Worked example

LISTENING TRACK 18

You are listening to a radio programme about customs in Spain. Answer the following question **in English**.
What **two** benefits are said to result from the custom discussed? **(2 marks)**

improves your health and helps you avoid stress

Listen to the recording

– Vamos a hablar de las costumbres de aquí. ¿Qué opinas de la siesta?

– Es cierto que la siesta forma parte de nuestras tradiciones desde hace mucho tiempo. Además, se dice que mejora la salud y que ayuda a evitar el estrés.

Listening strategies

When you are listening to a conversation, pay particular attention to the questions, as they will guide you to the information you need to complete the task successfully.

Here you need to understand that **mejora la salud** means 'improves your health'. Even if you didn't recognise the verb **mejorar**, you could make the link to the word **mejor**, meaning 'better'.
El estrés is a cognate that is easy to pick out. If you don't remember the verb **evitar**, you can make a sensible guess that it would help avoid stress.

Now try this

LISTENING TRACK 19

Now listen to the rest of the programme from the worked example. Answer the following questions **in English**.

(a) Where has this tradition been lost? **(1 mark)**

(b) What has been proved in the past by scientific studies? **(1 mark)**

Listen to the recording

Spanish festivals

Revise vocabulary on this topic so you can understand descriptions of festivals in Spain.

Fiestas

España es famosa por sus fiestas.
Spain is famous for its festivals.

Algunas son de naturaleza religiosa y otras son históricas.
Some are religious in character and others are historical.

Muchas se celebran cada año.
Many are celebrated every year.

Tienen lugar ...   They take place ...
 al aire libre.   in the open air.
 en el centro urbano.   in the city centre.
 en las aldeas /   in the small villages.
  los pueblos.

Las calles están cerradas al tráfico.
The streets are closed to traffic.

Es una tradición popular.
It's a popular tradition.

Hay fuegos artificiales.   There are fireworks.

Mucha gente participa en desfiles.
A lot of people take part in processions.

La gente se viste con trajes tradicionales.
People are dressed in traditional clothes.

Mucha gente baila.   Lots of people dance.

Using se to avoid the passive

The passive voice ('is celebrated', 'was celebrated', etc.) is used frequently in English but is often avoided in Spanish by using the reflexive pronoun se.

La fiesta se celebra una vez al año.
The festival is celebrated once a year.

This translates literally as: The festival celebrates itself once a year.

The reflexive pronoun agrees with the subject.

Se llevan trajes de flamenco.
Flamenco costumes are worn.

Se lanzan tomates.   Tomatoes are thrown.

El pueblo se convierte en ...
The village becomes ...

La famosa Feria de Abril se celebra en Sevilla.
The famous April fair is celebrated in Seville.

La ciudad se llena de música y ruido.
The town is filled with music and noise.

Worked example

SPEAKING

Prepare your answers to these points.

1 ¿Qué hay en la foto?
En esta foto se ve una fiesta tradicional con muchos fuegos artificiales magníficos. En la foto hay mucha gente y parece un espectáculo fantástico. A mí me encantaría ir a esta fiesta. ...

2 ¿Qué piensas de las fiestas?
Para mí las fiestas son muy importantes porque nos dan la oportunidad de entender más de la cultura de un lugar y de formar parte de un grupo grande de gente de varias edades. Además son muy divertidas. ...

3 Describe una fiesta a la que
El año pasado mi familia y yo fuimos a una fiesta tradicional del pueblo pequeño donde vivo. Se cerraron las calles al tráfico y bailamos mucho. ...

Exam alert

When you are preparing your answers to the questions on the photo card, try to anticipate what the two unexpected questions might be and have some ideas ready. Here are two examples:
– ¿Piensas que gastan demasiado dinero en las fiestas en España?
– ¿Hay aspectos negativos de las fiestas?

Now try this

SPEAKING
TRACK 20

Talk about the photo in the worked example. Include information for each of the bullet points. Also answer these questions:

4 ¿Por qué piensas que hay tantas fiestas en España?

5 ¿Qué fiesta española te gustaría ver?
Try to talk for three and a half minutes.

Listen to the recording

South American festivals

Prepare to describe and write about festivals in Spanish-speaking countries in South America.

Las actividades festivas

La gente prepara platos especiales.
People prepare special dishes.
Decoran la casa.   They decorate the house.
Las familias se reúnen.   Families get together.
Organizan juegos y concursos.
They organise games and competitions.
Todo el mundo se acuesta tarde.
Everyone goes to bed late.
Hay música y baile en las calles.
There is music and dancing in the streets.
el Día de los Muertos
the Day of the Dead (All Soul's Day)
El ambiente en las calles es genial.
The atmosphere on the streets is great.

La gente se disfraza de
fantasmas y esqueletos.
People dress up as ghosts
and skeletons.

Using haber in various tenses

The verb haber is used in different tenses to express 'there is', 'there will be' etc. It is always used in the third person singular and hay is the special form that haber takes in the present tense.
Hay un baile en la plaza.
There is a dance in the square.
Habrá una procesión a las diez.
There will be a procession at ten o'clock.
Cada año había espectáculos de fuegos artificiales.
Every year there were firework displays.
Pensé que habría problemas de seguridad.
I thought there would be safety issues.

Worked example

 WRITING

Translate this passage **into Spanish**.   **(12 marks)**

> Last autumn I went to see my relatives in Mexico and we took part in the activities for the Day of the Dead. My aunt made some special dishes and all the family came to visit. It is an exciting festival and there is a lively atmosphere. Next year, my cousin will come to my house for Christmas.

El otoño pasado fui a ver a mis parientes en México y tomamos parte en las actividades del Día de los Muertos. Mi tía hizo unos platos especiales y toda la familia vino a visitar. Es una fiesta emocionante y hay un ambiente animado. El año que viene, mi primo vendrá a mi casa para Navidad.

Exam alert

The translation will contain some straightforward sections and also some more challenging parts. You can get round the tricky bits by expressing an idea in a different way. For example, if you can't remember the irregular verb hizo (he/she made) you could use the regular verb preparó (he/she prepared).

Now try this

WRITING

Translate the following passage **into Spanish**.   **(12 marks)**

> The bullfight is a Spanish tradition that is also celebrated in many South American countries. I went to visit the bullring in Mexico last year and I watched a bullfight. I didn't like it at all but the atmosphere was very exciting and it was a new experience. I will not go again.

Describing a region

Use this page to enable you to describe the region where you live.

Mi región

Mi región es tranquila. My region is quiet.

Mi barrio es ruidoso.

My neighbourhood is noisy.

La zona es residencial.   The area is residential.

El paisaje es bonito.   The scenery is beautiful.

Es una provincia industrial.

It's an industrial province.

Hay pocos habitantes.

There are not many inhabitants.

Vivo en las afueras de la ciudad.

I live in the suburbs / outskirts.

Los alrededores son preciosos.

The surrounding area is beautiful.

Los bosques son pintorescos.

The woods are picturesque.

La torre fue construida hace doscientos años.

The tower was built two hundred years ago.

Antes había muchos bloques de pisos.

There used to be lots of tower blocks.

Ahora tiene más zonas verdes.

Now it has more green spaces.

Connectives

Use connectives to help you structure your opinions.

además	also, as well, moreover
por un lado …	on the one hand …
por otro lado …	on the other hand …
en realidad / de hecho	actually / in fact
aparte de	apart from
a pesar de esto	in spite of this
es decir	that is to say / I mean
sin duda	without a doubt

Parece una región histórica con muchos edificios impresionantes y, sin duda, es un lugar tranquilo.

It seems like a historic region with many impressive buildings and it is, without doubt, a peaceful area.

Worked example

READING

Lee el artículo.

La provincia de Cádiz

El diverso carácter de la provincia de Cádiz está marcado por su gente, su bahía y su historia. En sus paisajes se aprecian grandes contrastes, desde el Campo de Gibraltar hasta la belleza de Jerez de la Frontera, sus pueblos blancos o las costas de Tarifa.

No se puede olvidar su capital, Cádiz, que tiene cultura y tradiciones que la diferencian del resto. Cádiz es sin duda el destino ideal para tus vacaciones.

En su costa atlántica destacan sus playas largas de arena fina. Muchas de ellas aún no están urbanizadas ni explotadas turísticamente.

¿Qué hay en la provincia?

A	playas y aldeas
B	bosques y montañas
C	ciudades industriales

Escribe la letra correcta en la casilla. [A]   **(1 mark)**

Exam alert

Escribe la letra correcta en la casilla means 'Write the correct letter in the box'. Learn other key instructions too:

Completa la tabla.

Fill in the table.

Contesta a las preguntas en español.

Answer the questions in Spanish.

Responde a todos los aspectos de la pregunta.

Answer all parts of the question (i.e. write something about each bullet point).

To choose the correct answer, rule out some options: woods and mountains are not mentioned and **Cádiz** is not described as industrial. Then make the connection between **aldeas** and **pueblos**.

Remember! Questions in Spanish require answers **in Spanish**.

Now try this

READING

Lee el artículo y contesta a las preguntas **en español**.

(a) Explica la diversidad de la provincia de Cádiz.   **(1 mark)**

(b) ¿Por qué se debe visitar la ciudad de Cádiz?   **(1 mark)**

Describing a town

This page will help you describe your town and talk about what you would like to change.

Descripción de mi ciudad

Mi ciudad se llama ...   My town is called ...

Está en el norte / este / sur / oeste de Inglaterra.
It is in the north / east / south / west of England.

Hay / Tiene doce mil habitantes.
There are 12,000 inhabitants.

En mi ciudad hay ...
In my town there is / are ...

muchos turistas.	lots of tourists.
muchas zonas de ocio.	lots of leisure areas.
una buena red de transporte público.	a good public transport network.
mucha contaminación.	lots of pollution.
muchos árboles.	lots of trees.
pocas tiendas de ropa.	few clothes shops.
pocas instalaciones.	few facilities.

En mi ciudad hay muchos espacios verdes.
In my town there are lots of green spaces.

The conditional tense
Grammar page 96

You use the conditional to talk about what you would do. To form it, add the following endings to the infinitive. Some verbs use a different stem, but the endings are the same for all verbs.

	hablar – to speak
I	hablaría
you	hablarías
he / she / it	hablaría
we	hablaríamos
you	hablaríais
they	hablarían

Construiría ...	I would build ...
Podría ...	I would be able to ...
Habría ...	There would be ...
Mejoraría ...	I would improve ...

Worked example
LISTENING TRACK 21

Listen to the recording. What does Héctor say about his town? Write the correct letter in the box.

A	Gandía is in the south-east of Spain.
B	There are over 70,000 inhabitants.
C	He would encourage more tourists to visit.
D	He would provide more green spaces.
E	Lanzarote has 150,000 inhabitants.
F	There are not enough buses in Lanzarote.
G	Laura thinks buses would improve daily life.
H	Looking after Lanzarote's natural resources is key.

☐ A   **(1 mark)**

– Vivo en Gandía, una ciudad que está en el sureste de España.

Listen to the recording

Listening strategies

- ✓ **Always** read the options before you listen. Identify key words and structures to listen out for.
- ✓ If you are confident of any answers on first listening, put a cross by those letters to reduce your options for the second listening.

Look at the sentences. What do you need to listen out for?
- Numbers (**sesenta**? no: **setenta**)
- Verbs in the conditional
- Key words: **turistas, autobuses, espacios verdes**, etc.

Now try this
LISTENING TRACK 22

Listen to the recording

Look at the worked example. Listen to the whole recording of Héctor and Laura speaking about where they live. Write the other **three** correct letters in these boxes.

☐ ☐ ☐

(3 marks)

Places to see

You need to know places in a town and you need prepositions to say where they are.

Los lugares de interés

Se puede ver ...	You can see ....
el ayuntamiento.	the town hall.
el museo.	the museum.
la galería de arte.	the art gallery.
el teatro.	the theatre.
la plaza de toros.	the bull ring.
la estación de tren.	the train station.
la iglesia.	the church.
la biblioteca.	the library.
la catedral.	the cathedral.
la mezquita	the mosque
el castillo.	the castle.
el palacio.	the palace.
los monumentos.	the monuments.
Hay muchas tiendas.	There are lots of shops.
la carnicería	the butcher's
la pescadería	the fishmonger's
la panadería	the baker's
la frutería	the fruit shop
el supermercado	the supermarket
la ferretería	the hardware store
el quiosco (de periódicos)	the newspaper stand
la farmacia	the chemist's

Prepositions

Use prepositions to describe location. Note that de + el changes to del.

Está ...

delante de in front of	detrás de behind	al lado de next to

entre between	cerca de near to	lejos de far from

enfrente de	opposite
a mano derecha / izquierda	on the right / left hand side
en la esquina	on the corner
a 10 minutos	10 minutes away

Está delante del cine.
It's in front of the cinema.

Worked example

READING

Read Martín's note about what he has to do.

lunes
Ir al supermercado para comprar bolígrafos para el instituto. Llevar libros a la biblioteca delante del banco y comprar una postal para José en la tienda del museo.

martes
Ir a la farmacia enfrente de la frutería a comprar perfume. Comprar entradas para la exposición de la galería de arte mañana. Mandar correo electrónico al banco. Por la noche comprar pan.

Answer the question in English.
Why is Martín going to the supermarket? **(1 mark)**
to buy pens for school

Exam alert

When answering questions in English, ensure you give all the relevant details. Martín is going to the supermarket to buy pens, but if you read on you will discover the pens are for school, so you should also include this information in your answer.

Now try this

READING

Read the text in the worked example and answer the questions **in English**.
(a) Where is Martín going to buy a postcard?

(1 mark)
(b) Where will he go first on Tuesday?

(1 mark)
(c) Where is he going on Wednesday?

(1 mark)
(d) What will he do last thing on Tuesday?

(1 mark)

Places to visit

This page gives more vocabulary for things to do in new places.

¿Qué van a hacer?

Vamos a ir ...	We are going ... / Let's go
a la piscina municipal.	to the public swimming pool.
al cine.	to the cinema.
al campo.	to the countryside.
al centro histórico.	to the historic district.
al centro de ocio.	to the leisure centre.
al mercado.	to the market.
al parque temático.	to the theme park.
al centro turístico costero.	to the seaside resort.
al parque zoológico.	to the zoo.

Se puede ...	You can ...
ver plazas y puentes.	see squares and bridges.
disfrutar de unas vistas maravillosas.	enjoy some marvellous views.
conocer la cultura.	experience the culture.
ver un espectáculo.	see a show.
ir a un partido.	go to a match.
ver exposiciones especiales.	see special exhibitions.

Using se puede to say what you can do

Se puede is an impersonal verb used to talk about what people in general can do. It is followed by the infinitive.

Se puede visitar un parque temático.
You can visit a theme park.
Se puede practicar muchos deportes.
You can do many sports.

Worked example

- ¿Qué lugares me recomendarías visitar como turista?
  Mi ciudad es muy interesante. Se puede visitar el museo y además hay muchos restaurantes y bares donde se puede comer tapas.

 AIMING HIGHER Se puede visitar el museo y así se conoce la cultura. A mí me encanta Bilbao porque se puede experimentar la cultura vasca. También se puede caminar por el casco antiguo y se puede ver un espectáculo de música vasca porque forma parte de su patrimonio cultural. ¿Usted ha visitado el casco antiguo de Bilbao?

Exam alert

In the general conversation part of your speaking exam, make sure that you **justify** a **wide range** of individual thoughts and opinions. It is a good idea to ask the examiner questions, to show that you are able to **sustain** and **lead** the conversation.

Aiming higher

Try to include the following features:
- ✓ a connective (así, porque, pero, etc.) to make a complex sentence
- ✓ opinion phrases (en mi opinión, me encanta)
- ✓ less common verbs (to show a wider range of vocabulary).

Now try this

Now give your own answer to the question in the worked example.

The weather

Use this page to prepare for understanding weather forecasts.

¿Qué tiempo hace?

Llueve / Está lloviendo.

Nieva / Está nevando.

Hace sol.

Hay niebla.

Hace calor.

Hace frío.

Hace viento.	It's windy.
el pronóstico del tiempo	weather forecast
el clima	climate
Hace mal / buen tiempo.	It's bad / good weather.
Está nublado.	It's cloudy.
Hay tormenta.	It's stormy.
Hay truenos.	There's thunder.
Hay relámpagos.	There's lightning.
seco/a	dry
lluvioso/a	rainy
caluroso/a	hot
soleado/a	sunny

Different tenses

Understanding the weather in different tenses is a higher-level skill.

Expressions with hacer	
Hacía calor.	It was hot.
Hará frío.	It will be cold.
Hará sol.	It will be sunny.
Expressions with estar	
Estaba nublado.	It was cloudy.
Expressions with haber	
Había niebla.	It was foggy.
Habrá tormenta.	It will be stormy.
nevar (to snow) and llover (to rain)	
Nevaba.	It was snowing.
Llovía.	It was raining.
Va a nevar / llover.	It's going to snow / rain.

Look out for time markers as a clue to the tense.

ayer	yesterday
hoy	today
mañana	tomorrow

Worked example

LISTENING TRACK 23

Listen to the recording. What is the forecast for Bilbao today? Write the correct letter in the box.

Listen to the recording

A	wind
B	sun
C	rain

[B] **(1 mark)**

– Bilbao, sábado 12 de marzo. Ayer llovía pero hoy hace sol. Mañana nevará.

Exam alert

You need to be secure with your verb tenses so that you can identify different time frames during a listening task.

The key word to listen out for here is **hoy** (today).

Now try this

LISTENING TRACK 24

Listen to the recording

Listen to the full recording from the worked example. Write the correct letter in each box.

(a) In Seville yesterday it was …

A	windy.
B	cold.
C	foggy.

(b) It will be windy …

A	tonight.
B	tomorrow.
C	on Saturday.

(c) Now the weather is …

A	hot.
B	stormy.
C	cloudy.

(3 marks)

Shopping

Use the language here to give your opinion about shopping.

Ir de compras

Me chifla ir de compras.
I love going shopping.
Odio los grandes almacenes.
I hate department stores.
Me encantan las tiendas pequeñas.
I love small shops.
No me gustan nada los centros comerciales.
I really don't like shopping centres.

el escaparate	the shop window
el probador	the changing room
la ropa	clothes
los guantes	gloves
los vaqueros	jeans
las joyas	jewellery
el brazalete / la pulsera	bracelet
las zapatillas de deporte	trainers

Mi número de zapato es el 42.
My shoe size is 42.
Busco un vestido de talla 38.
I am looking for a size 38 dress.

Direct object pronouns
Grammar page 07

	Masculine	Feminine
it	lo	la
them	los	las

– Estos zapatos son demasiado pequeños.
– Lo siento, no los tengo en su número.

Aiming higher

Try to use direct object pronouns in your spoken and written Spanish to create more complex statements.
Odio usar los probadores pero es difícil evitarlos en las tiendas de ropa.
I hate using changing rooms but it's hard to avoid them in clothes shops.

Worked example

Lee el artículo sobre comprar por Internet.

Las ventajas de comprar por Internet son claras: se evita hacer colas y también, con solo hacer clic, se puede comprar artículos que no se encuentran en tu país. Pero comprar por Internet también tiene sus desventajas. Algunas de ellas son los pagos, la devolución de los artículos y el ser víctima de fraude. A pesar de todo esto, es posible que en un futuro no muy lejano la mayoría de nuestras compras se hagan de esta forma. Lo importante es que los consumidores tengan tanto cuidado en el mundo virtual como en el mundo real.

Answer the question in English.
Mention **two** advantages of buying online.   **(2 marks)**
avoiding queues / finding items not in your country

¿Cuál es una de las ventajas de comprar por Internet?

A	Los precios son más bajos.
B	Hay seguridad total.
C	Puedes comprar cosas del extranjero.

Escribe la letra correcta en la casilla.   C   **(1 mark)**

The key to knowing that C is correct is understanding the phrase **comprar artículos que no se encuentran en tu país**. Make sure you learn as much higher-level vocabulary as possible.

Now try this

Lee el artículo otra vez. Según el texto, ¿qué hará mucha gente en el futuro? Escribe la letra correcta en la casilla.

A	Visitará más tiendas virtuales.
B	Gastará más dinero en centros comerciales.
C	No querrá hacer compras por internet.

☐   **(1 mark)**

Buying gifts

Be prepared to describe gifts, using colours and other adjectives.

Los regalos

los recuerdos	souvenirs
el maquillaje	make-up
el perfume	perfume
una barra de labios	a lipstick
un cinturón	a belt
un sombrero	a hat
una gorra	a cap
una pelota	a ball
un disco compacto / un CD	a CD
un videojuego	a computer game
una consola de juegos	a games console
unos calzoncillos	boxer shorts
una corbata	a tie
una sudadera	a sweatshirt
unas zapatillas de deporte	trainers
de algodón	(made of) cotton
de cuero / de piel	(made of) leather
de lana	(made of) wool

Colours

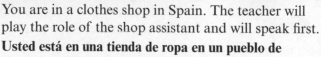

verde   negro   amarillo   rosa

rojo   blanco   marrón   azul

Demonstrative adjectives

Grammar page 86

Demonstrative adjectives (this, that, these, those) are used with a noun and must agree with that noun.

	Masculine	Feminine
this / these		
Singular	este	esta
Plural	estos	estas
that / those		
Singular	ese	esa
Plural	esos	esas

este reloj   this watch
esta camiseta   this T-shirt

estas botas   esos zapatos
these boots   those shoes

Worked example

SPEAKING

You are in a clothes shop in Spain. The teacher will play the role of the shop assistant and will speak first.

Usted está en una tienda de ropa en un pueblo de España y quiere comprar algo.

1 Ropa – tipo
  Hola. ¿En qué puedo ayudarle?
  Me gustaría comprar una gorra.

2 Color preferido
  Muy bien. Tenemos varios colores. ¿Cuál prefiere?
  Prefiero una gorra roja.

3 ? Precio
  ¿Cuánto cuesta la gorra?
  Son veinte euros.

4 !
  Habla bien el español. ¿De dónde es usted?
  Soy de Escocia.

5 Pueblo – opinión
  Muy bien. ¿Le gusta este pueblo?
  Sí, me gusta mucho porque es muy pintoresco y bastante pequeño.

Exam alert

Remember: when asked for an opinion in a role play, you need to justify your opinion!
Me gusta mucho porque es muy pintoresco y bastante pequeño.

This candidate has chosen to buy a cap for the gift. As **una gorra** is feminine, the colour needs to agree – **una gorra roja**. If the candidate had chosen a masculine item, such as a belt, it would have been **un cinturón rojo**.

Now try this

SPEAKING
TRACK 25

Now prepare your own answers to the role play prompts in the worked example. Listen to the track of the teacher's part and speak your answers in the pauses.

Listen to the recording

Money

Topics concerning money always involve numbers. Make sure you know them.

El dinero

Gano nueve euros por hora en la bolera.
I earn nine euros an hour at the bowling alley.

Recibo una paga semanal de mis padres.
I receive weekly pocket money from my parents.

Ahorro dinero.   I save money.

Lo pongo en la caja de ahorros.
I put it in the savings bank.

Recargo el saldo del móvil cada quince días.
I buy credit for my mobile every fortnight.

Me lo gasto en ...   I spend it on ...

revistas   caramelos   ropa

maquillaje   pendientes   libros / novelas

Direct object pronouns
Grammar page 87

Use direct object pronouns to avoid repeating a noun.

¿Te gustan los caramelos?
  Sí, los compro cada quince días.
Do you like sweets?
  Yes, I buy them every fortnight.

Recibo dinero de mis padres.
  Lo ahorro para descargar música.
I get money from my parents.
  I save it to download music.

The pronoun agrees in number and gender with the noun it replaces:

	Singular	Plural
Masculine	el dinero ➡ lo	los libros ➡ los
Feminine	la ropa ➡ la	las novelas ➡ las

Worked example

LISTENING TRACK 26

Listen and answer the question **in English**.   **(2 marks)**
What does she not spend her pocket money on?
make-up or concert tickets

Listen to the recording

– Mis hermanas se lo gastan en maquillaje o entradas para conciertos, pero yo no.

Remember to listen out carefully for negatives. It's when she talks about her sisters that she tells us what she does **not** buy.

Exam alert

In the exam you won't be able to control the audio as you can in this book! Instead, the listening recording for each numbered question will be played twice with a short pause between hearings. After the second playing, there will be a longer pause for you to write your answer before the next question is heard.

If a question is divided into several parts (for example, 6.1, 6.2, 6.3, …) then all the parts refer to the same extract and you must listen for all the answers in one go before the whole extract is played again.

In question (a), the verb forms to listen out for are conditional or future, as she will talk about her future plans.

Now try this

LISTENING TRACK 27

Listen to the whole recording from the worked example and answer the questions **in English**.

(a) Why is she saving her money?   **(1 mark)**

(b) What did she use to do with her money?   **(2 marks)**

(c) Why won't she get pocket money from her parents next year?   **(1 mark)**

Listen to the recording

Charities

Be prepared for understanding texts about charitable causes and fundraising.

La caridad

una fundación benéfica	a charitable foundation
una campaña global	a worldwide campaign
una organización benéfica	a charitable organisation
Es a / en beneficio de ...	It's in aid of ...
recaudar fondos	to fundraise
organizar una venta benéfica	to organise a charity sale
asistir a una venta de pasteles	to attend a cake sale
participar en una carrera	to take part in a race

publicar los eventos benéficos en las redes sociales
to publicise charity events on social media

Doy dinero porque ...	I give money because ...
me importa.	it matters to me.
puedo hacer una diferencia.	I can make a difference.
quiero ayudar a los demás.	I want to help others.
me gustaría mejorar la vida de los demás.	

I would like to make other people's lives better.

Using Ojalá to say 'Let's hope!'

Grammar page 99

Ojalá is a word which means 'let's hope' or 'if only'. You need to use the subjunctive after this word.
Ojalá la situación mejore.
Let's hope the situation improves.
Ojalá pudiera correr un maratón.
If only I could run a marathon.

Use expressions like these in your writing and speaking if you want to aim for a high grade.

Worked example

Lee el texto y completa la frase.
Escribe la letra correcta en la casilla.
La organización trabaja en muchos ...

A	niños	E	colegios
B	personas	F	campañas
C	pobres	G	enfermos
D	países	D	**(1 mark)**

When completing the gaps in an exercise, make sure your answer not only makes sense, but also is grammatically correct. For example, in question (b) you are looking for an adjective, not a noun.

Save the Children

Trabajamos para que millones de niños tengan la oportunidad de ser lo que quieren ser hoy, de soñar lo que serán mañana y de construir un mundo mejor. Llegamos a 55 millones de niños gracias a las 25.000 personas que trabajan en más de 120 países. Actualmente uno de cada tres niños en España está en riesgo de pobreza o exclusión social. La infancia de nuestro país es el colectivo que más está sufriendo las consecuencias del desempleo y de los recortes en las ayudas sociales. Por ello, centramos nuestro trabajo en España en luchar contra la pobreza infantil. La educación es la herramienta más poderosa para romper el ciclo de transmisión de la pobreza de padres a hijos.

Now try this

Lee el texto otra vez y completa las frases con la palabra correcta. Escribe la letra correcta en cada casilla.

(a) Hay veinticinco mil .... que trabajan para la organización. ☐ **(1 mark)**

(b) Ahora hay más niños españoles .... debido a la crisis económica. ☐ **(1 mark)**

(c) Trabajan en .... para cambiar la situación en España. ☐ **(1 mark)**

Volunteering

Use this page to prepare for understanding texts about volunteering.

El voluntariado

Trabajé de / como voluntario/a ...
I worked as a volunteer ...

Trabajamos sin cobrar ...
We worked without pay ...

Me ofrecí como voluntario ...
I became a volunteer ...

en una clínica.
in a clinic.

en un instituto.
in a school.

en una residencia de ancianos.
in an old people's home.

en zonas de conflicto.
in conflict zones.

al aire libre.
in the open air.

Hay muchas ventajas en este tipo de trabajo.
There are many advantages to this type of work.

Puedes aprender muchas habilidades nuevas.
You can learn lots of new skills.

Puedes adquirir experiencia en el área que te interese.
You can gain experience in the area you are interested in.

Es bueno ayudar a los más necesitados.
It is good to help those most in need.

Talking generally using 'you'

To talk generally about what someone **can** do, use the verb poder in the tú form in the present tense:
Puedes vivir una experiencia única.
You can experience something unique.

Or in the future tense:
Podrás trabajar con niños.
You will be able to work with children.

Or use it in the él/ella form with the impersonal pronoun se:
Se puede conocer a todo tipo de personas.
You can get to know all types of people.

Use the verb deber to say what someone **should** do. You can use the conditional tense with the tú form:
Deberías dedicar tu tiempo a los démas.
You should dedicate your time to others.

Or, to sound more formal, use the conditional tense of deber in the él/ella form with pronoun se:
Se debería ofrecer tiempo para ayudar a los demás.
You should offer time to help others.

Worked example

LISTENING TRACK 28

Listen to the recording

Listen to Juan. Which **two** opinions about volunteering does he express?

A	It is hard work.
B	It makes you feel good.
C	It can teach you work skills.

D	It is now more popular.
E	It is not for everyone.

Write the correct letters in the boxes. [B] [C]   **(2 marks)**

– El voluntariado es bueno para los demás, pero también para uno mismo. Aunque no esté remunerado, puedes realizar tareas que tengan relación con tu carrera profesional o puesto de trabajo; esto te ayudará a ganar experiencia para futuros trabajos.

The vocabulary surrounding this topic is quite difficult. However, use your deductive skills to pick out key words and phrases in order to answer successfully: **para uno mismo** (for oneself), **ganar experiencia** (to gain experience) **para futuros trabajos** (for future jobs).

Now try this

LISTENING TRACK 29

Listen to the recording

Listen to the whole recording from the worked example and answer the questions **in English**.

(a) What will volunteering help you with?   **(1 mark)**

(b) When did Juan volunteer?   **(1 mark)**

(c) What did Juan gain from the experience?   **(1 mark)**

(d) What is his opinion about his own voluntary work?   **(1 mark)**

Helping others

Be prepared to talk about how you help other people or how you would like to help.

Ayudar a otros

¿Por qué se debería ayudar a otros?
Why should you help other people?
Es bueno ser generoso y amable.
It's good to be generous and kind.
Si haces cosas buenas por los demás te sentirás mejor contigo mismo.
If you do good deeds for other people you will feel better about yourself.
Para ayudar a otras personas …
To help other people …
  visito a los ancianos en una residencia.
  I visit the elderly in a care home.
  voy de compras para mis vecinos.
  I go shopping for my neighbours.
  ayudo a mi hermana con sus deberes.
  I help my sister with her homework.
  trabajo en el jardín de mi abuelo.
  I help in my granddad's garden.
  voy de paseo con el perro de mi abuela.
  I take my grandmother's dog for a walk.

The imperfect tense

Grammar page 94

Remember to use the imperfect when you describe what you used to do, as well as the following time phrases:

antes	before
a menudo	often
siempre	always
nunca	never
todos los días / cada día	every day

Antes no ayudaba mucho a mis padres pero ahora lavo el coche cada sábado.
I did not use to help my parents much but now I wash the car every Saturday.

Worked example

Lee el artículo.

¿Ayudas a los demás?

Es importante ayudar a tu familia a menudo; ofrecer ayuda con las tareas domésticas o con tareas de cualquier otro tipo. Ayudar es especialmente importante cuando ves que algún miembro de tu familia o de tus amigos parece estresado o está muy ocupado, son estas personas las que realmente van a apreciar tu ayuda. Observa como se sienten tus familiares y piensa en lo que puedes hacer para hacerles la vida mas fácil.

¿Qué tipos de tareas puedes hacer por ellos?

Pues una de las más fáciles, y de las más agradecidas, es preparar una comida para ellos o ir al supermercado a comprar los ingredientes necesarios para un buen almuerzo o cena. Hacer la compra y cocinar para los demás es un acto generoso y especialmente útil si alguien, aunque no esté ocupado, no se encuentra bien.

¿Y ayudar a hermanos o primos más pequeños? Ofrece hacer de canguro y así das un descanso bien merecido a sus padres. Tu ayuda será recompensada con gran agradecimiento y reconocimiento. ¡Te sentirás genial!

Contesta a la pregunta **en español**.
¿Cuándo es bueno ofrecer ayuda a un amigo? **(1 mark)**
Cuando parece estresado / cuando está muy ocupado

To help you find the answer, you need to read the first two sentences carefully. The text states that you should help your family often (**es importante ayudar a tu familia a menudo**) but mentions helping friends when they are stressed or busy (**cuando ves que algún miembro de tu familia o de tus amigos parece estresado o está muy ocupado**)

Now try this

Lee el artículo otra vez y contesta a las preguntas **en español**.
(a) ¿Qué puedes hacer para ayudar a alguien que no se siente bien? **(1 mark)**
(b) ¿Cómo puedes ayudar a los familiares con niños? **(1 mark)**

Healthy living

Use this page to prepare yourself to talk about healthy food and a healthy lifestyle.

La vida sana

llevar una vida activa	to lead an active life
acostarse	to go to bed
dormirse	to go to sleep
el entrenamiento	training
hacer deporte	to do sport
hacer ejercicio	to do exercise
una dieta equilibrada	a balanced diet
estar / mantenerse en forma	
to be / to keep fit	
evitar	to avoid
la salud	health
sano / saludable	healthy
el pescado	fish
la carne	meat
las verduras	vegetables
la fruta	fruit
la leche	milk
el agua	water

Es bueno para la salud.
It's good for the health.
No contiene mucha grasa.
It doesn't contain much fat.

Using gustar and encantar

These verbs that we use for 'to like' and 'to love' are used differently from other verbs.

I like fish.   Me gusta el pescado.
(This literally means 'fish pleases me')

I like vegetables.
Me gustan las verduras.
(This literally means 'vegetables please me')

I love fruit.   Me encanta la fruta.
I love oranges.   Me encantan las naranjas.

Other useful phrases:
Me gusta mucho.
I like it a lot.
Me gusta bastante.
I quite like it.
No me gusta nada.
I don't like it at all.

Me gusta llevar una vida activa.
I like to lead an active life.

 **Worked example**

Prepare your answers to the bullet points.

1 ¿Qué hay en la foto?

En la foto hay una familia que come a la mesa. Es una comida muy sana porque toman una ensalada y diferentes tipos de fruta.

2 ¿Qué haces tú para llevar una vida activa?

En mi tiempo libre me gusta hacer deporte y el domingo pasado, jugué al tenis con mi hermano. Mañana iré a la piscina porque me encanta la natación. Cuando hago ejercicio, me siento más sano.

3 ¿Qué comida sana comiste ayer?

Ayer comí una sopa de verduras y tomé una ensalada de pollo. Bebí un zumo de naranja.

This learner shows off their knowledge of different tenses: jugué, iré, hago (preterite, future, present) which will allow them to achieve more highly in the 'range of language' category.

The third question is in the preterite, asking what healthy food you ate yesterday. Ensure you answer using the same tense.
I ate – comí
I had – tomé
I drank – bebí
I tried – probé
I made – hice

 Now try this   TRACK 30

Listen to the recording

Prepare your own answers to the questions in the worked example and the two questions below, which are the unexpected questions. Then listen to the track and speak your answers in the pauses.

4 ¿Cómo vas a mejorar tu dieta en el futuro?

5 ¿Qué otros aspectos son importantes para tener una vida sana?

Unhealthy living

Use this vocabulary to talk about unhealthy lifestyles.

Los malos hábitos

malsano	unhealthy
hacer daño	to do harm, damage
fumar	to smoke
dejar de fumar	to stop smoking
el cigarrillo	cigarette
el humo	smoke
respirar	to breathe
el tabaquismo	tobacco addiction
beber alcohol	to drink alcohol
emborracharse	to get drunk
estar borracho/a	to be drunk
las drogas blandas	soft drugs
las drogas duras	hard drugs
el porro	joint / spliff
drogarse	to take drugs
la tentación	temptation
estar enfermo/a	to be ill
el cuerpo	body
el corazón	heart
el hígado	liver
los pulmones	lungs
oler	to smell
huele mal	it smells bad
el olor	smell
el sida	AIDS
el sobrepeso	overweight, obesity

Using deber, hay que and tener que

Use the present tense of deber for 'must'.
Los jóvenes nunca deben tomar drogas.
Young people must never take drugs.

Use the conditional for 'should' or 'ought'.
Los adultos deberían beber alcohol con moderación.
Adults should drink alcohol in moderation.

Use hay que + infinitive for 'we must', 'you must' or 'one must'.
Hay que resistir la tentación de fumar.
One must resist the temptation to smoke.

Use tener que + infinitive for 'to have to'.
Tengo que perder unos kilos.
I have to lose a few kilos.

Hay que cuidar el cuerpo.
You must look after your body.

Listen to the recording

Worked example

LISTENING TRACK 31

Pablo talks about his family's lifestyle. What is the problem with each member of the family?

A	drinks too much	D	is overweight
B	smokes	E	does no exercise
C	takes drugs	F	does not get enough sleep

Listen to the recording and write the correct letter in the box.

(a) Pablo's father B   **(1 mark)**

– Mi padre todavía fuma y me preocupa mucho porque a veces le resulta difícil respirar.

Exam alert

There is usually more than one clue to the answer to give you some help in case you miss one of the words or don't know a certain item of vocabulary. For example, in this exercise, if you were to hear: Mi hermano es un poco gordo porque come demasiadas patatas fritas. Necesita perder unos kilos, the words for 'fat', 'chips' and 'lose kilos' would all point you to the correct answer.

Now try this

LISTENING TRACK 32

Listen to the recording

Listen to the rest of the recording from the worked example and write the correct letter in each box.

(b) Pablo's mother ☐   (c) Pablo's brother ☐   (d) Pablo's sister ☐   **(3 marks)**

Peer group pressure

Use the language here to help you write about peer group influences.

La presión del grupo

Puede ser una influencia positiva o negativa.
It can be a positive or negative influence.

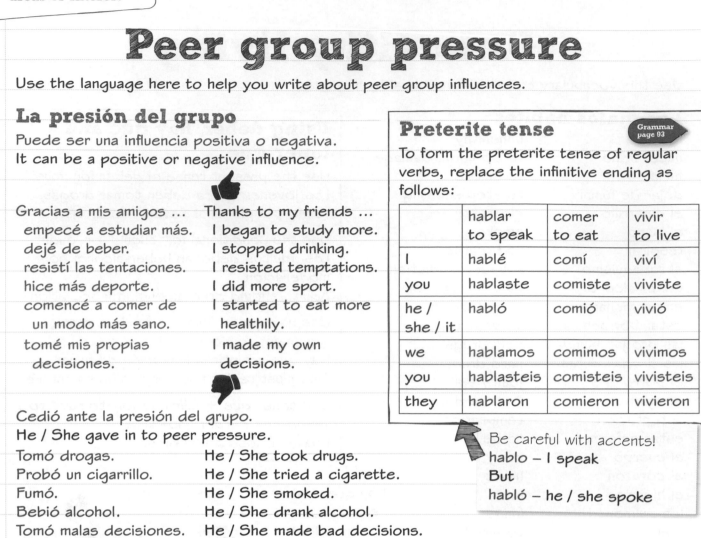

Preterite tense
Grammar page 93

To form the preterite tense of regular verbs, replace the infinitive ending as follows:

	hablar to speak	comer to eat	vivir to live
I	hablé	comí	viví
you	hablaste	comiste	viviste
he / she / it	habló	comió	vivió
we	hablamos	comimos	vivimos
you	hablasteis	comisteis	vivisteis
they	hablaron	comieron	vivieron

Be careful with accents!
hablo – I speak
But
habló – he / she spoke

Gracias a mis amigos …   Thanks to my friends …
empecé a estudiar más.   I began to study more.
dejé de beber.   I stopped drinking.
resistí las tentaciones.   I resisted temptations.
hice más deporte.   I did more sport.
comencé a comer de   I started to eat more
un modo más sano.   healthily.
tomé mis propias   I made my own
decisiones.   decisions.

Cedió ante la presión del grupo.
He / She gave in to peer pressure.
Tomó drogas.   He / She took drugs.
Probó un cigarrillo.   He / She tried a cigarette.
Fumó.   He / She smoked.
Bebió alcohol.   He / She drank alcohol.
Tomó malas decisiones.   He / She made bad decisions.

Worked example

Escribe de sobre
• tus experiencias de presión del grupo.

AIMING HIGHER

El mes pasado cedí ante la presión del grupo y empecé a fumar cigarrillos. Lo hice para ser aceptado pero en realidad lo odiaba. Es una estupidez y esta semana dejé de fumar porque no quiero caer en el hábito de hacerlo cada día como algunos de mis amigos. A partir de ahora, intentaré tomar mis propias decisiones.

Aiming higher

Try to include the following features in your writing:
✓ a range of tenses (present, preterite, imperfect, future)
✓ a good number of less common verbs (ceder, empezar, dejar)
✓ a variety of connectives (y, pero, como)
✓ object pronouns (lo hice – I did it).

Now try this

Escribe un artículo sobre la amistad. Menciona:
• una descripción de un/a amigo/a
• las cualidades de un buen amigo
• tus experiencias recientes de presión del grupo
• los planes para el futuro que tenéis tú y tu mejor amigo/a.

Escribe aproximadamente **90** palabras **en español**. Responde a todos los aspectos de la pregunta. **(16 marks)**

Green issues

Make sure you know vocabulary relating to the environment.

Los problemas medioambientales

Los problemas más graves son ...
The most serious problems are ...

la contaminación / la polución	pollution
la destrucción de la capa de ozono	
the destruction of the ozone layer	
el cambio climático	climate change
el calentamiento global	global warming
las inundaciones	floods
la destrucción de la selva tropical	
the destruction of the rainforest	
el aumento de las sequías	
the increase in droughts	
las especies en peligro de extinción	
species in danger of extinction	
la falta de recursos naturales	
the lack of natural resources	
la contaminación de los océanos	
pollution of the oceans	
la basura	rubbish
el planeta	the planet
los terremotos	earthquakes

Phrases with the subjunctive

Grammar page 99

Learn some expressions that use the subjunctive to improve your speaking and show you can use complex structures.
Use the present subjunctive after these expressions:

Es importante que ...	It's important that ...
Es esencial que ...	It's essential that ...
Es increíble que ...	It's incredible that ...
Es terrible que ...	It's terrible that ...

Es importante que separemos la basura.
It's important that we sort our rubbish.

Worked example

- ¿Cuáles son los problemas más graves del planeta?

   Para mí, el problema más grande es el calentamiento global. Pienso que deberíamos usar más el transporte público y reutilizar más productos.

AIMING HIGHER
Es esencial que trabajemos contra la destrucción de la capa de ozono si queremos salvar nuestro planeta. Es necesario que reciclemos más. No deberíamos malgastar electricidad ni consumir tanta energía. Además, es importante que compremos pilas recargables y reutilicemos bolsas de plástico.

This is a satisfactory answer but it could be improved.

Here various tenses are used effectively, as well as the subjunctive:
Es esencial que trabajemos ... ,
Es necesario que reciclemos ...
The use of connectives and conjunctions such as **si** and **además** also helps raise the level.

Speaking strategies

Try not to use English sounds when you hesitate, such as 'um' or 'er'. Instead, fill any gaps with Spanish equivalents – pues, a ver, es decir.

Now try this

- ¿Cuáles son los problemas más graves del planeta?

Natural resources

Make sure you learn a range of vocabulary about looking after the planet.

Los recursos naturales

cuidar la tierra	to look after the earth
proteger el campo	to protect the countryside
convertir en abono	to compost
evitar el malgasto de ...	to prevent wasting ...
consumir	to consume
el consumo	consumption
reciclar	to recycle
el reciclaje	recycling
reutilizar	to reuse
ahorrar	to save, economise
la electricidad	electricity
el carbón	coal
la energía	energy
la energía solar	solar power
el gas	gas
el petróleo	oil
el agua dulce	fresh water
el agua salada	salt water
la pesca	fishing

The perfect tense

Grammar page 97

At Foundation level, you need to know the most common verbs in the perfect tense.

He usado el transporte público en Londres.
I have used public transport in London.

At Higher level, you need to know how to use the perfect tense of a wider range of verbs, including irregular verbs.

He puesto el vidrio en el contenedor de reciclaje.
I have put the glass in the recycling container.

Ahorro energía / electricidad.
I save electricity.

Worked example

READING

Lee el texto.
Contesta a la pregunta **en español**.
¿Qué organizó el instituto?
(1 mark)

Un concurso para ayudar al medio ambiente.

El mes pasado, el instituto San Lorenzo de Calatayud decidió lanzar un concurso entre sus estudiantes para diseñar una campaña medioambiental que tuviera un impacto verdadero en los alrededores. El director, José Salinas, nos explicó la iniciativa: 'En lugar de estar sentados en el aula, los estudiantes tenían que crear un proyecto que, al final de una semana, ayudase al medio ambiente de alguna manera evidente.'

Uno de los grupos montó un quiosco delante de un gran supermercado y vendió bolsas de tela a los clientes para evitar el consumo de más bolsas de plástico. Otro grupo colocó contenedores especiales en cada clase para recoger botellas de plástico y al final de la semana las llevó a una empresa de reciclaje. El grupo que ganó el premio para la idea más innovadora fue el que escribió un pequeño libro de recetas que da ideas sobre cómo usar los restos de comida. El libro incluye ideas para una tortilla muy sabrosa y varias sopas deliciosas.

Now try this

READING

Contesta a las preguntas **en español**.
(a) ¿Qué hizo el primer grupo? **(1 mark)**
(b) ¿Qué hizo el segundo grupo con las botellas? Menciona dos razones. **(2 marks)**
(c) ¿Qué contiene el libro? **(1 mark)**

Environmental action

Learn how to use 'if' clauses so you can use them in the writing exam.

Proteger el medio ambiente

Se debe ría ...	You should ...
No se debe ría...	You should not ...
evitar	avoid
correr el riesgo de	run the risk of
aumentar	increase
reducir	reduce
malgastar	waste
dedicarse a	devote time to
intentar	try to
lograr	achieve
pre ocuparse de	to be concerned with
ponerse a	start
quejarse de	complain about
usar el transporte público	use public transport
apagar las luces	turn off the lights
proteger la naturaleza	protect nature
separar la basura	recyle your rubbish
usar bolsas de plástico	use plastic bags
en vez de	instead of

'If' clauses

In clauses with si (if), you need to use the correct verb forms:

☑ Si + present tense + future tense

Si no malgastamos la energía, será mejor para el medio ambiente. If we don't waste electricity, it will be better for the environment.

☑ Si + imperfect subjunctive + conditional

Si todo el mundo se dedicara a no usar bolsas de plástico, no habría tanto residuo tóxico. If everyone tried not to use plastic bags, there would not be as much toxic waste.

Worked example

Escribe un texto sobre el medio ambiente. Menciona:
- lo que haces para proteger el medio ambiente.

Quiero proteger el planeta y por eso siempre separo la basura. Reciclo el vidrio, el papel y el plástico y siempre uso los contenedores correctos.

 AIMING HIGHER

Sin duda me pre ocupo mucho del medio ambiente. Mi familia siempre compra productos ecológicos, ya que no contienen productos químicos malos. He comprado un bonobús, así que puedo usar el transporte público a menudo y es barato. Claro que es mejor que viajar en coche todo el tiempo. Si más gente fuese a pie o en autobús, reduciríamos la contaminación del aire.

This piece of writing has a good range of verb forms:
- compra, contienen ➡ present
- he comprado ➡ perfect
- fuese ➡ imperfect subjunctive
- reduciríamos ➡ conditional

It also contains some interesting conjunctions, **ya que** and **así que**, as well as connectives such as **claro que** and **sin duda**.

Now try this

Escribe un artículo sobre el medio ambiente. Menciona:
- por qué es importante proteger el medio ambiente
- lo que has hecho recientemente para proteger el medio ambiente.

Escribe aproximadamente **150** palabras **en español**. Responde a todos los aspectos de la pregunta.   (**32 marks**)

Global issues

Be prepared to talk about important issues affecting the world.

Los problemas globales

los desastres naturales — natural disasters
la falta de agua potable — lack of drinking water
el hambre mundial — world hunger
la guerra — war
los derechos humanos — human rights
los necesitados — the disadvantaged
la pobreza — poverty
la crisis económica — the economic crisis
el crimen en Internet — internet crime

los 'sin techo'
homeless people

Key verbs for expressing ideas

Use these key verbs to help you discuss serious global issues.

compartir — to share
darse cuenta de — to realise
enseñar — to teach
investigar — to research
mostrar — to show
notar — to note
parar — to stop
tratar de — to try to

En mi opinión, tenemos que tratar de parar el hambre mundial.
In my opinion we have to try to end world hunger.

Worked example

Read the text.

Los problemas globales son aquellos que afectan los intereses de toda la comunidad mundial, que amenazan el futuro de la humanidad, que atentan contra las posibilidades de desarrollo de la civilización. Entre los problemas globales que tradicionalmente se incluyen en diferentes listados se encuentran los siguientes: la gran desproporción en los niveles de desarrollo social y económico entre las distintas partes del planeta, las amenazas a la seguridad y la paz internacional, la problemática ecológica, y el agotamiento de los recursos naturales no renovables.

How does the text describe global problems? Write the correct letter in the box.

A	always environmental
B	increasing substantially
C	a danger to our existence

C (1 mark)

Unfamiliar words

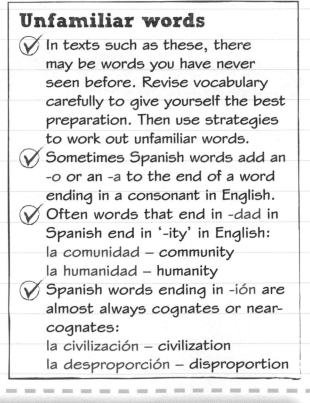

- ✓ In texts such as these, there may be words you have never seen before. Revise vocabulary carefully to give yourself the best preparation. Then use strategies to work out unfamiliar words.
- ✓ Sometimes Spanish words add an -o or an -a to the end of a word ending in a consonant in English.
- ✓ Often words that end in -dad in Spanish end in '-ity' in English:
la comunidad – community
la humanidad – humanity
- ✓ Spanish words ending in -ión are almost always cognates or near-cognates:
la civilización – civilization
la desproporción – disproportion

Now try this

Read the text in the worked example again. What global problems are mentioned? Write the correct letter in the box.

A	threats to our security and green issues
B	poverty and crime
C	violence and lack of drinking water

(1 mark)

Poverty

If you are aiming for a higher grade, make sure you are able to understand more complex texts about global issues.

La pobreza

arruinar	to ruin
el aumento de	the increase in
combatir	to combat, fight
los derechos	rights
la desigualdad	inequality
echar la culpa a	to put the blame on
la escasez de	the shortage of
la falta de	the lack of
limpio	clean
sucio	dirty
el gobierno	government
los necesitados	the needy
los pobres	the poor
el hambre	hunger
la sed	thirst
pasar frío y hambre	to go cold and hungry
grave	serious
injusto	unfair
inquietante	alarming
preocupante	worrying
me preocupa que ...	it worries me that ...
me inquieta que ...	it concerns me that ...
me enfada que ...	it annoys me that ...

Using the subjunctive after verbs of emotion

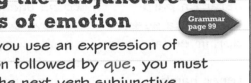
Grammar page 99

When you use an expression of emotion followed by que, you must make the next verb subjunctive.

Me preocupa que haya tanta pobreza en el mundo.
It worries me that there is so much poverty in the world.

Me enfada que el gobierno no haga suficiente para ayudar.
It annoys me that the government does not do enough to help.

Me inquieta que muchos niños tengan que pasar hambre y sed.
It concerns me that many children have to go hungry and thirsty.

Worked example

LISTENING TRACK 33

Listen to the recording

Listen to this conversation in a Spanish classroom about problems in a developing country. Answer the question **in English**.

What is Martín's main worry?   **(1 mark)**

The drought has ruined the food they were growing.

– Sobre todo me preocupa que la sequía haya arruinado la comida que cultivaban.

Exam alert

With the more challenging listening texts, you may be required to pick out just one opinion from a range of possibilities. If you are asked for the **main** concern or the **worst** problem, this may mean that more than one issue is mentioned and you must listen out for the right one. Listen out for key phrases like sobre todo (above all), el problema principal (the main problem), lo más preocupante (the most worrying thing), which will lead you to the correct answer.

Now try this

LISTENING TRACK 34

Listen to the recording

Listen to the rest of the recording from the worked example and answer the questions **in English**.

(a) What problem does Rosa think will cause disease?   **(1 mark)**
(b) What does Julio think is a scandal?   **(1 mark)**
(c) What does Cristina see as the main problem?   **(1 mark)**

Homelessness

Use this page to prepare for understanding texts about the social problem of homelessness.

Los 'sin techo'

pedir ayuda	to ask for help
estar en paro	to be unemployed
tener mala suerte	to have bad luck
dormir en las calles	to sleep on the streets
tener hambre	to be hungry
estar enfermo	to be ill
morir	to die
depender de actos solidarios	to depend on acts of charity
ayudar a + infinitive	to help to …
vestirse con ropa vieja	to dress in old clothes
cubrirse de periódicos	to cover oneself in newspapers
el prejuicio	prejudice
nada que comer	nothing to eat

Verbs that take a following preposition

Many verbs are followed by a preposition which must be inserted before the next noun or infinitive.

Se cubren de periódicos para evitar el frío.
They cover themselves in newspapers to keep out the cold.
Les ayudamos a encontrar alojamiento.
We help them to find accommodation.
Dependen de actos solidarios.
They depend on acts of charity.
Tienen que pedir ayuda.
They have to ask for help.

Se visten con ropa vieja.
They dress in old clothes.

Worked example

READING

You read this entry on a website forum.

En mi barrio hay un grupo de hombres 'sin techo' que viven bajo el puente del ferrocarril. Para vivir, dependen de actos solidarios y me preocupa que no tengan nada que comer esta Navidad. Me enfada que el ayuntamiento no haga nada para ayudarlos. Ahora hay esperanza. Unos amigos de mis padres han comprado una tienda vacía y van a convertirla en un comedor para los necesitados. Allí servirán comida caliente, y los visitantes podrán descansar un rato en un café con calefacción y un poco de espíritu navideño.   *Fernando*

Answer the question **in English**.
Where do the homeless men live?   **(1 mark)**
under the railway bridge

It is important to be able to recognise vocabulary wherever it appears as most of the words you come across can appear in several topics. Here, for example, there are words like puente, ferrocarril and ayuntamiento, which are from the Home, town and neighbourhood topic.

Aiming higher

Test your vocabulary by choosing a topic (like la pobreza) and writing down as many Spanish words as you can that relate to that issue. For example: pobre (poor), necesitado (needy), hambre (hunger), 'sin techo' (homeless) …

Now try this

READING

Read the text again. Answer the questions **in English**.
(a) What is Fernando worried about?   **(1 mark)**
(b) What have his parents' friends just bought?   **(1 mark)**
(c) What are they going to turn it into?   **(1 mark)**
(d) What will they serve?   **(1 mark)**
(e) What other benefit will the visitors gain? Mention **one** thing.   **(1 mark)**

Countries and nationalities

Remember to be accurate with your adjective endings when describing nationalities.

Países y nacionalidades

Soy de / Vivo en …	I'm from / I live in …
África / Asia / Europa	Africa / Asia / Europe
América del Norte / Norteamérica	North America
América del Sur / Sudamérica	South America
América Latina / Latinoamérica	Latin America

País		Nacionalidad
España		español
Inglaterra		inglés
Escocia		escocés
Gales		galés
Irlanda		irlandés
Grecia		griego
Francia		francés
Alemania		alemán
Suiza		suizo
Estados Unidos		americano

In Spanish, nationalities **don't** have a capital letter.

Talking about nationalities

Like other adjectives, adjectives of nationality agree.

	Singular	Plural
Nationalities ending -o:		
Masculine	suiz<u>o</u>	suizos
Feminine	suiza	suizas
Nationalities ending in a consonant:		
Masculine	inglé<u>s</u>	ingleses
Feminine	inglesa	inglesas

When you talk about people from a country, you always use the definite article.
Me gustan los españoles.
I like Spanish people.

Nationalities with an accent on the ending lose it in feminine and plural forms, e.g.
escocés   escoceses   escocesa

Worked example

WRITING

Escribe a tu amigo/a español/a sobre ti. Menciona:
- tu nacionalidad
- dónde naciste.   **(10 marks)**

AIMING HIGHER

Nací en Suiza aunque desde hace diez años vivo en Inglaterra porque mis padres trabajan aquí. Mi madre es alemana pero nació en Dinamarca, así que soy mitad suizo y mitad alemán. Me gustan los ingleses, por lo tanto en el futuro viviré en Londres.

Aiming higher

✓ The best answer will use the bullet points to show off knowledge of a **range of tenses**. This candidate uses present, preterite and future to describe his nationality, and varies the **verb endings** to give information about his family too.

✓ Using **connectives** (aunque, porque, pero, así que, por lo tanto) makes your writing more coherent and more interesting.

Now try this

WRITING

Write about your own nationality. Aim to write at least **40** words.   **(16 marks)**

Tourist information

Make sure you know the vocabulary for asking about tourist attractions.

En la oficina de turismo

¿Tiene ... ?	Do you have ... ?
un mapa de la región	a map of the region
una lista de hoteles	a list of hotels
una lista de albergues juveniles	a list of youth hostels
un folleto de excursiones	a brochure about trips
un horario de trenes / autobuses	a train / bus timetable

Quiero información sobre ...
I'd like information about ...
una visita guiada (a pie)   a (walking) tour

¿Qué hay de interés en ... ?
What is there of interest in ... ?

¿A qué hora abre / cierra el museo?
What time does the museum open / close?

Hay ...   There is ...
Se puede ...   It's possible ... / You can ...
Merece / Vale la pena ver ...   It's worth seeing ...

Si yo fuera usted, visitaría ...
If I were you, I would visit ...

Lo interesante es que se puede ...
The interesting thing is that you can ...

Question words

Grammar page 103

¿Dónde?	Where?
¿Adónde?	Where to?
¿Cuánto?	How much?
¿Cuándo?	When?
¿A qué hora?	At what time?
¿Qué?	What?
¿Cómo?	How?
¿Cuál?	Which?

lo + adjective

Use lo + adjective to refer to an abstract idea.

lo bueno	the good thing
lo malo	the bad thing
lo aburrido	the boring thing
lo interesante	the interesting thing

There is also a superlative form:
Lo más interesante es que hay playas bonitas.
The most interesting thing is the beautiful beaches.

Worked example

READING

Translate this passage **into English**.   (4 marks)

Estoy de vacaciones en Mallorca y las playas son tan bonitas. Fui a la oficina de turismo y ...

I am on holiday in Mallorca and the beaches are so beautiful. I went to the tourist information centre and ...

Exam alert

You have to translate a passage from Spanish to English as part of the reading exam.
You will be marked on communication and accuracy, so make sure that your translation communicates the meaning of the passage and that it flows well.

You often need to change the word order when translating so that your English text makes sense. For example, translate las playas bonitas as 'pretty beaches', not 'beaches pretty'!

Now try this

READING

Translate the rest of the passage **into English**.   (5 marks)

... encontré mucha información, como por ejemplo, el horario de autobuses. Mañana haré una visita guiada a pie por el centro de la ciudad con mis padres.

Accommodation

This page will help you to say more about holidays and to express your opinions.

El alojamiento

Me estoy alojando en …	I am staying in …
Me alojo en …	I stay in …
un camping	a campsite
un hotel de cinco estrellas	a five-star hotel
un albergue juvenil	a youth hostel
una pensión / un hostal	a guest house
nuestro apartamento en Francia	our flat in France
alquilar	to hire, rent
una caravana	a caravan
un piso alquilado	a rented flat
una casa	a house
Prefiero quedarme en un hotel.	I prefer staying in a hotel.

Using me gusta(n) and me encanta(n)

Grammar page 101

Me gusta (I like) literally translates as 'it pleases me'. The thing that does the pleasing (i.e. the thing I like) is the subject. If this subject is plural, use me gustan.
Me gusta dormir al aire libre.
I like sleeping outdoors.

Me encanta behaves in the same way.
Me encanta alquilar un apartamento.
I love renting a flat.

And to say what you don't like …
No me gusta quedarme en un camping.
I don't like staying on a campsite.

Aiming higher

Using quedarse as well as alojarse in the **preterite** and **future** will show off your knowledge of the language.

me quedé / me alojé	I stayed
me quedaré / me alojaré	I will stay

me gusta ♥
me gusta mucho ♥ ♥
me encanta ♥ ♥ ♥

Worked example

SPEAKING

Estás hablando con tu amigo español sobre las vacaciones.

1 ¿Qué hay en la foto?

AIMING HIGHER En esta foto se ve a una familia que está de vacaciones en un camping con su caravana.

2 ¿Qué piensas de las vacaciones en un camping?
No me gusta nada pasar las vacaciones en un camping porque siempre es muy incómodo dormir en una tienda. Además, muchas veces los servicios están sucios o las duchas no funcionan.

3 Háblame de la última vez que fuiste de vacaciones.
Normalmente voy a un camping bastante aburrido pero el año pasado me quedé en un hotel precioso de cinco estrellas.

Speaking strategies

In the picture-based tasks, you will be asked a question for each of the bullet points. Remember that as part of this task you will also have to answer two unexpected questions. Use the preparation time to make notes on key verbs and tenses that you will use for each bullet point.

You will need the conditional to describe your ideal holidays. Rather than just saying me gustaría, try to vary the verbs you use: iría a … , me alojaría en … .

Now try this

Listen to the recording

Work out your own answers to the points in the worked example and the two points here also.
Listen to the audio track here and speak your answers in the pauses. Try to talk for at least three minutes.

4 ¿Qué planes tienes para las vacaciones este año?   5 Háblame de tus vacaciones ideales.

Hotels

Be prepared to take part in conversations about booking accommodation.

En un hotel

Quiero reservar ...	I'd like to book ...
una habitación individual / doble.	a single / double room.
sin baño.	without a bathroom.
con ducha / balcón.	with a shower / balcony.
¿Para cuántas noches?	For how many nights?
para siete noches	for seven nights
¿A qué hora se sirve / sirven el desayuno / la cena?	What time is breakfast / dinner served?
¿Está incluido el desayuno?	Is breakfast included?
¡Disfrute su estancia!	Enjoy your stay!
completo	full
con vistas al mar / a la piscina / a la montaña	with a sea / pool / mountain view
la recepción	reception
la llave	key
el ascensor	lift
media pensión	half board
pensión completa	full board
conexión a Internet	internet connection
quince días	fortnight

Revising numbers
Grammar page 105

You can never review numbers too often! Here are a few ideas:

✓ **Look at** the numbers on page 105.
Can you identify any patterns that will help you remember them?
– 16 to 19 are dieci + 6, dieci + 7, etc.
– 31, 41, 51, etc. are always y uno (but 21 is different)
– tres / trece / treinta

✓ **Practise** numbers on your own: count in twos, in threes, in fives. Count backwards! Or practise playing bingo with a friend!

Worked example

You are in a hotel in Spain. The teacher will play the part of the receptionist and speak first.

Estás en un hotel en España. Estás hablando con el/la recepcionista. Quieres reservar una habitación.

1 Habitación – tipo
   Buenos días. ¿En qué puedo servirle?
   Quiero una habitación doble con ducha, por favor.

2 Noches – número
   Muy bien. ¿Para cuántas noches?
   Me gustaría la habitación para cinco noches.

3 !
   ¿Prefiere una habitación con vistas al mar o a la montaña?
   Prefiero una habitación con vistas al mar.

4 Planes – una actividad para mañana
   De acuerdo. ¿Tiene planes para mañana?
   Sí, vamos a visitar el castillo y luego nos gustaría ir a un restaurante típico.

5 ? Desayuno – precio
   ¿El desayuno está incluido en el precio de la habitación?
   Sí, está incluido.

Exam alert

Role play strategies
This topic lends itself very well to a role play. Use the preparation time for the speaking exam to read the role play prompts carefully and to decide what you will say for each one. Remember that you can reuse the vocabulary from the prompt. For example:
Habitación – tipo ➡
Quiero una habitación doble. (I want a double room.)

Now try this

Prepare your own answers to these role play prompts. Listen to the recording of the teacher parts and fill in your parts in the pauses.

1 Habitación – tipo
2 Noches – número
3 !
4 Planes – una actividad para mañana
5 ? Desayuno – precio

Listen to the recording

Camping

Learn the vocabulary here to help you understand texts about campsites.

El camping

¡Vamos a acampar!	Let's camp!
el camping	the campsite
Está en el campo.	It's in the countryside.
una tienda	a tent
una caravana	a caravan
un cubo para basura	a rubbish bin
una piscina cubierta	an indoor pool
una lavandería (automática)	a launderette
una tienda de comestibles	a grocery shop
una sala de juegos	a games room
un cajero automático	a cash machine
las duchas	the showers
la ropa de cama	bed linen
un saco de dormir	a sleeping bag
el alquiler de bicicletas	bike hire

Es obligatorio apagar las luces a medianoche.
It is compulsory to turn off the lights at midnight.

No se permite hacer ruido.
Being noisy is not allowed.

No se permiten animales.
Animals are not allowed.

Using different verbs

To make your writing and speaking more varied, don't just use different tenses – use different verbs too. Make lists in diagrams like this:

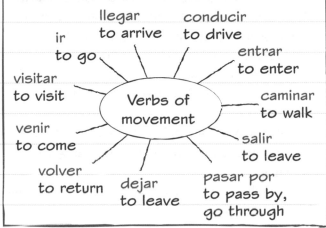

- llegar to arrive
- conducir to drive
- ir to go
- entrar to enter
- visitar to visit
- caminar to walk
- Verbs of movement
- venir to come
- salir to leave
- volver to return
- dejar to leave
- pasar por to pass by, go through

Note: Use **se permite** if it refers to a single thing, but **se permiten** if it refers to more than one thing.

Worked example

Read the texts.

En el camping
- El horario de silencio es de 01.00 a 07.00. Durante estas horas, se prohíbe la circulación de vehículos.
- No se permite hacer carreras de bicicletas.
- Están prohibidos los juegos de pelota cerca de las tiendas.
- El volumen o sonido de los aparatos de televisión debe ser, durante todo el día, lo más bajo posible.

En el albergue juvenil
- No se permite hacer ruido después de medianoche.
- No se permite comer en los dormitorios.
- Es obligatorio traer el saco de dormir.
- Es obligatorio utilizar los cubos para basura.

Reading strategies

Students perform well in tasks like this when they have a good knowledge of basic vocabulary items and use deductive reasoning. Use your ability to think, as well as your knowledge of Spanish!

What are you allowed to do in the campsite?

A	play ball games throughout the site
B	drive your car at 8am
C	race bicycles

Write the correct letter in the box. ☐B☐ **(1 mark)**

To answer this question correctly, you need to use the context of the texts and take advantage of the cognates to deduce that **circulación de vehículos** means 'driving vehicles'.

Now try this

Now read the texts from the worked example again and answer the questions **in English**.

(a) What are you told about TVs on the campsite? **(1 mark)**

(b) Which **two** things is it compulsory to do in the youth hostel? **(2 marks)**

Holiday preferences

This page will help you express your opinions on holidays in lots of different ways.

Prefiero las vacaciones ...

😊	😞
Prefiero las vacaciones en la playa con amigos.	No me gusta ir de vacaciones con mis padres.
I prefer holidays on the beach with friends.	I don't like going on holiday with my parents.
Mis vacaciones ideales serían en el Caribe.	No soporto hacer camping.
My ideal holidays would be in the Caribbean.	I can't stand going camping.
Es maravilloso conocer una ciudad y perderme por las calles estrechas.	Odio los sitios ruinosos por el turismo descontrolado.
It's wonderful getting to know a city and losing myself in the narrow streets.	I hate places ruined by uncontrolled tourism.
Siempre he querido visitar Australia.	Me da vergüenza el comportamiento de los turistas británicos.
I have always wanted to visit Australia.	I am ashamed of the behaviour of British tourists.
Es relajante descansar sin pensar en el instituto.	Odio el sol porque siempre me pongo rojo.
It's relaxing to take it easy without thinking about school.	I hate the sun as it always makes me red.
	Me aburren los museos y la historia.
	Museums and history bore me.

Worked example

WRITING

Describe tus vacaciones ideales.

> Mis vacaciones ideales serían en España. Diría que las vacaciones en España sin padres son fenomenales pero ellos lo pagan todo, así que con padres no están tan mal.

AIMING HIGHER

> Mis vacaciones ideales serían en Italia. Podría visitar las ciudades famosas como Florencia y Roma. Me apasionan el arte y los museos. Además, la comida es excelente. Creo que tardaré muchos años en ir a Italia porque a mis padres les gusta el sol, así que tenemos que ir a la playa como todos los británicos. ¡Me da tanta vergüenza su comportamiento!

This question allows the use of the **conditional** to say what your favourite type of holiday would be.

This answer includes a variety of tenses and complex phrases (**me da vergüenza**). It also expresses different opinions.

Aiming higher

Try to include **more complex** language.
Mis padres siempre quieren que vaya con ellos.
My parents always want me to go with them.
Si pudiera, iría a Ibiza para ir de fiesta.
If I could, I'd go to Ibiza to party.

Now try this

WRITING

Escribe un artículo sobre las vacaciones perfectas. Menciona:

- adónde prefieres ir de vacaciones
- lo que no te gusta hacer de vacaciones
- lo que hiciste el año pasado de vacaciones
- adónde irás de vacaciones el próximo año y por qué.

Escribe aproximadamente **90** palabras **en español**. Responde a todos los aspectos de la pregunta.   **(16 marks)**

Holiday destinations

Make sure you know the future tense in order to talk about where you will go on holiday.

Adónde ir de vacaciones

Iré ...	I will go ...
a la costa.	to the coast.
a la montaña.	to the mountains.
a la playa.	to the beach.
al campo.	to the countryside.
a lugares culturales.	to cultural sites.
Descansaré.	I will rest.
Nadaré.	I will swim.
Haré yoga.	I will do yoga.
Iré a clases de baile.	I will go to dance classes.
Haré una excursión en bicicleta.	I will go on a cycling tour.
Veré lugares de interés.	I will see places of interest.
Montaré a caballo.	I will go horseriding.
Patinaré.	I will skate.
Esquiaré.	I will ski.
Haré alpinismo.	I will go rock / mountain climbing.
Haré vela.	I will go sailing.

The future tense
Grammar page 95

To form the future tense of most verbs, add the following endings to the infinitive:

	ir – to go
I will go	iré
you will go	irás
he / she / it will go	irá
we will go	iremos
you will go	iréis
they will go	irán

¿Adónde irás de vacaciones el año que viene?
Where will you go on holiday next year?
Iré a Grecia y haré una excursión en bicicleta.
I'll go to Greece and I'll go on a cycling tour.

Worked example WRITING

Escribe una carta a tu amigo español. Menciona:
• los planes para tus próximas vacaciones.

  Esquiaré en Francia con mi instituto. Va a ser genial. Nos quedaremos en un hotel cerca de la montaña.

 AIMING HIGHER

  El año que viene iré a la costa de Italia con mi novio. Creo que va a ser perfecto porque serán nuestras primeras vacaciones juntos. Descansaremos en la playa y mi novio dará una vuelta en bicicleta. A mi me encantan los caballos, así que montaré a caballo todos los días.

Using the **future** and the **near future** shows variety of tense usage. Adding more **detail** (where you will stay) can improve the content.

• Extending opinions by justifying them using connectives (**y, porque**) will help you if you are aiming higher.
• You can also use interesting phrases to show your grasp of a wider range of vocabulary, e.g. **nuestras primeras vacaciones juntos** (our first holiday together).

Now try this WRITING

Write your own response to the bullet point in the worked example about your holiday plans for next year. Write about 30–40 words.

(10 marks)

Travelling

As well as revising ticket vocabulary, make sure you know your numbers for times and prices.

Comprar billetes

Quiero dos billetes para...	I would like two tickets to ...
un billete de ida	a single ticket
un billete de ida y vuelta	a return ticket
para hoy / mañana	for today / tomorrow
¿A qué hora sale / llega?	What time does it depart / arrive?
Es directo.	It's direct.
un bonobús	a bus pass
¿Cuánto cuesta?	How much does it cost?
¿Hay descuento para los jóvenes?	Is there a discount for young people?
¿Cuánto tiempo dura el viaje?	How long does the journey take?
Dura ...	It takes ...
el próximo / último tren	the next / last train
Acaba de llegar / salir.	It has just arrived / departed.

Using para and por for 'for'

> Grammar page 102

Use these rules to work out whether to use para or por.

Por – cause
Gracias por su ayuda. Thanks for your help.
Por – expressing rates
Vuelos a Madrid por 50 euros. Flights to Madrid for 50 euros.
Para – purpose
Quiero un billete de ida para visitar a mi abuela. I want a single ticket to visit my grandmother.
Para – a destination
Salió para Granada. He left for Granada.
Para – period of time in the future
Quiero una habitación para una semana. I would like a room for a week.

Worked example

LISTENING TRACK 37

Listen to the conversation at the train station.
What does the man want?

Listen to the recording

A	a single ticket
B	a return ticket
C	a ticket for tomorrow

Write the correct letter in the box. [A]   **(1 mark)**

– Quiero un billete de ida para Sevilla para hoy.

Listening strategies

Students often find multiple-choice questions tricky, as it's easy to be put off by the wrong answers.
- ☑ Look at the options carefully before you listen.
- ☑ Try to predict what you are going to hear.
- ☑ Revise numbers and times, as they crop up in many contexts!

Now try this

LISTENING TRACK 38

Listen to the recording

Listen to the whole conversation from the worked example and write the correct letter in each box.

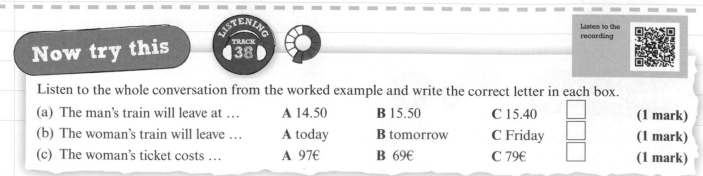

(a) The man's train will leave at ...   A 14.50   B 15.50   C 15.40   ☐   **(1 mark)**

(b) The woman's train will leave ...   A today   B tomorrow   C Friday   ☐   **(1 mark)**

(c) The woman's ticket costs ...   A 97€   B 69€   C 79€   ☐   **(1 mark)**

Holiday activities

Be prepared to talk about a wide range of activities that you enjoy doing on holiday.

Las actividades de vacaciones

¿Qué haces normalmente cuando estás de vacaciones?
What do you normally do on holiday?
Voy con mi familia / mis amigos a la playa.
I go with my family / friends to the beach.
Descanso / me relajo.   I relax.
Saco fotos.   I take photos.
Pinto y dibujo.   I paint and I draw.

Learning vocabulary

☑ Make yourself flashcards to help you memorise vocabulary – Spanish on one side and English (or a picture) on the other.
☑ Write notecards to help you prepare for assessments – write key words and phrases, structures and verb forms under topic headings.

Me baño en el mar.

Voy a discotecas.

Hago excursiones.

Hago esquí.

Hago surfing.

Hago piragüismo.

Monto en bicicleta.

Worked example

SPEAKING

• ¿Qué haces normalmente cuando estás de vacaciones?
Voy a Portugal con mis amigos. Es divertido porque vamos a discotecas. Nunca voy con mis padres porque es un rollo.

AIMING HIGHER
Siempre voy de vacaciones con mi hermana. Tiene dos años más que yo, por lo que tenemos los mismos gustos. El año pasado fuimos a Ibiza. ¡Fue estupendo! Nos bañamos en el mar y descansamos en la playa. Por las noches íbamos a las discotecas y bailábamos hasta las tres de la mañana. Yo creo que a mis padres les gustaría que fuéramos con ellos pero sería aburrido.

Speaking strategies

☑ Students who use a lot of words which are the same in English will only impress if they pronounce them in the correct Spanish way.
☑ Make sure you've learned a good range of vocabulary – filling your conversation with English words is not a good idea.

Now try this

SPEAKING

Answer this question. Talk for about one minute.
• ¿Qué haces normalmente cuando estás de vacaciones?

Review the **present tense** (see page 88) to prepare yourself for this topic. Don't just revise 'I' forms – be ready to talk about what your friends and family do on holiday too, and what you do together.

Holiday experiences

Make sure you know how to use the preterite tense, so you can talk about your experiences.

Vacaciones pasadas

¿Adónde fuiste de vacaciones el año pasado?
Where did you go on holiday last year?

el verano pasado	last summer
hace dos años	two years ago
Fui con mi familia / con mis amigos / solo/a.	I went with my family / with my friends / alone.
Me alojé / Me quedé …	I stayed …
Viajé en …	I travelled by …
Hice un intercambio.	I did an exchange.
Pasé una semana allí.	I spent one week there.
Hice un viaje con el instituto.	I went on a school trip.

Preterite tense

Grammar page 93

These verbs in the preterite will be useful for talking about past holidays.

	visitar – to visit	comer – to eat	salir – to go out
I	visité	comí	salí
you	visitaste	comiste	saliste
he / she / it	visitó	comió	salió
we	visitamos	comimos	salimos
you	visitasteis	comisteis	salisteis
they	visitaron	comieron	salieron

Useful verbs in the preterite for talking about holidays include:

vi	I saw
bebí	I drank
hice	I did
fue	it was
tuve	I had

Bebí un zumo de naranja.
I drank an orange juice.

Worked example

READING

Read this extract from the novel *Donde aprenden a volar las gaviotas* by Ana Alcolea where Arturo is talking about his summer holidays spent in Norway.

Dos días después de mi llegada, aquella ciudad me parecía aburrida: a las cinco de la tarde ya estaba todo cerrado y no había casi nadie por las calles de nuestro barrio, que estaba a las afueras. Cada trayecto de autobús costaba veinticinco coronas, o sea, tres euros, y pedalear hasta el centro en bicicleta no tenía ninguna gracia, así que entre el enfado que llevaba por no estar con el resto de mi familia en la playa y cierta sensación de no hacer nada, lo estaba pasando fatal. Nadie en la casa podia hablar y entender mi idioma. El padre de Erik, el superprofesor, me miraba como si fuera un bicho raro: no concebía que a mis quince años todavía no fuera capaz de seguir una conversación en inglés, como hacía allí todo el mundo a esa edad. Me metía en mi habitación, intentaba estudiar, aprender frases para luego emplearlas con la familia; pero, claro, aquello no funcionaba.

Answer the following question **in English**.

When did Arturo start to find the town boring? **(1 mark)**

Two days after his arrival

Reading literary texts strategies

✓ If you find literary passages difficult, don't be put off so that you give up. There may be difficult sections in it but you may not need to understand these sections to answer the questions. The questions will only target parts of the extract where the vocabulary is what you can reasonably be expected to cope with.

The Spanish word for 'boring' is very well known – **aburrido** – so skim read until you find the word in the text. Then try to read **around** the word. The answer is likely to be in the words just before or just after the key item of vocabulary 'boring'. In this case, the beginning of the sentence, before **aburrido**, gives us the answer: **dos días después de mi llegada** – two days after my arrival.

Now try this

READING

Read the extract again. Answer the following questions **in English**.

(a) What was the town like at five o'clock in the afternoon? Arturo mentions **two** things. **(2 marks)**

(b) What **two** forms of transport could Arturo use to get into the town centre? **(2 marks)**

(c) What **two** things were people in the house unable to do? **(2 marks)**

Transport and directions

Use this vocabulary to talk about transport and understand or give directions.

El transporte

¿Vas a pie o en coche?
Do you walk or go by car?

Normalmente voy ...	Normally I travel ...
en coche.	by car.
en metro.	by underground.
en tren.	by train.
en barco.	by boat.
en moto.	by motorbike.
en ciclomotor.	by moped.
en autocar.	by coach.
en avión.	by plane.
la parada de autobús	bus stop
la vía para bicicletas	cycle path
el alquiler de coches	car hire
la zona peatonal	pedestrian zone
la conexión / el enlace	connection / junction

El viaje dura una hora.
The journey takes an hour.

El metro está muy cerca.
The underground station is very close.

Prefiero coger el autobús.
I prefer to catch the bus.

Odio andar / ir a pie.   I hate walking.

Me gusta viajar en avión pero es caro.
I like to travel by plane but it is expensive.

Giving directions

You will need to understand and give directions.

→ Dobla a la derecha.

← Dobla a la izquierda.

↑ Sigue todo recto.

Toma la primera calle a la izquierda.

Toma la segunda calle a la derecha.

Toma la tercera calle a la derecha.

Cruza el puente.

Pasa el semáforo.

- Note cojo – I catch.
- el for all transport except la bicicleta / la moto.
- en coche (by car), etc. but a pie (on foot).

Worked example

Listen to the conversation with Lucía and answer the following question **in English**.

How does Lucía prefer to go to school?   **(1 mark)**

walking

– Hola Lucía, ¿cómo vas al instituto?
– Generalmente voy en coche pero prefiero ir andando.

Exam alert

Remember that you do not need to answer in full sentences.

Make sure that you can recognise verbs in different forms, such as the gerund, e.g. andando (walking).

Now try this

Now listen to the whole conversation from the worked example and answer the following questions **in English**.

(a) Why does she prefer to walk to school?   **(1 mark)**

(b) What does she sometimes do?   **(1 mark)**

Transport problems

You will need to deal with problems linked to travelling and transport.

Problemas de transporte

Hay grandes retrasos.   There are long delays.

Los semáforos no funcionan.
The traffic lights are not working.

Los atascos son peores que el año pasado.
The traffic jams are worse than last year.

Hay demasiados camiones.   There are too many lorries.

Hemos perdido el vuelo.   We have missed the flight.

El aparcamiento está lleno.   The car park is full.

Mi coche no tiene gasolina.   My car has no petrol.

¿Qué pasó?   What happened?

Tuvieron un accidente ...   They had an accident ...
  en la autopista.   on the motorway.
  en la carretera.   on the road.
  en la calle.   in the street.

Hubo una colisión entre diez vehículos.
There was a crash involving ten vehicles.

Un peatón cruzó la calle sin mirar.
A pedestrian crossed the street without looking.

No ha habido / hubo heridos.   No one was injured.

How to say 'because of'

In Spanish, there are several ways to describe what has caused an event or situation:

✓ a causa de   because of
A causa de una huelga en Francia no hay vuelos a Paris.
Because of a strike in France there are no flights to Paris.

✓ debido a   due to
Debido a una tormenta en Nueva York, el vuelo IB6789 va con retraso.
Due to a storm in New York flight IB6789 is delayed.

✓ gracias a   thanks to
Gracias a Iberia, llegaré a tiempo.
Thanks to Iberia, I will arrive on time.

El conductor no vio al ciclista.
The driver did not see the cyclist.

Worked example

READING

Read the texts about recent accidents.
Who was delayed by two hours?

A	Alejandro
B	Belén
C	Carlos
D	Daniela

Write the correct letter in the box.

[C]   (1 mark)

Alejandro: Fue horrible. Hubo una colisión entre un camión grande y dos peatones en la calle cerca de mi casa.

Belén: Ayer vi un accidente en la carretera. No hubo heridos pero había un retraso de veinte minutos debido a eso.

Carlos: En la autopista hubo un accidente muy grave entre dos coches. Llevaron a los conductores al hospital, y después de marcharse la ambulancia, estuvimos dos horas en un atasco enorme.

Daniela: Siempre hay muchos accidentes en la carretera principal cerca de mi instituto a causa de los coches que van demasiado rápido.

Now try this

READING

Read the text in the worked example again. Write the correct letter in each box.
You can use each letter more than once.

(a) Who saw an accident but no one was hurt?   ☐   (1 mark)

(b) Who describes an accident involving a lorry?   ☐   (1 mark)

(c) Who thinks people drive too fast?   ☐   (1 mark)

(d) Who writes about a motorway crash?   ☐   (1 mark)

(e) Who mentions that pedestrians were involved in an accident? ☐   (1 mark)

When choosing the correct person for a reading task, you must read **all** of the texts before you begin to look for **specific details** mentioned in the statements.

Holiday problems

Lots of things can go wrong on holiday! Make sure you know how to say them in Spanish.

En el hotel

Quiero quejarme.	I want to complain.
La luz no funciona.	The light does not work.
El aire acondicionado no funciona.	
The air conditioning does not work.	
No hay calefacción.	There is no heating.
No hay toallas.	There are no towels.
Necesito dos almohadas.	I need two pillows.
La habitación no está limpia.	
The room is not clean.	
Me hace falta papel higiénico / jabón.	
I need toilet paper / soap.	
El baño / El aseo está sucio.	
The bathroom / toilet is dirty.	

Falta una cucharita.   There's a teaspoon missing.

No está bien hecho.   It is not cooked properly.

¿Me puede traer unas servilletas?

Please can you bring me some napkins?

No hay ni aceite ni vinagre.

There is no oil or vinegar.

La comida está demasiado salada.

The food is too salty.

Using the verb faltar

Some Spanish verbs are only used in the **third person** singular and plural. Faltar is the verb to use if something is missing or needed. You use the plural form when you need more than one thing.

Falta una cuchara.

There's a spoon missing.

Faltan un cuchillo y un tenedor.

There's a knife and fork missing.

You can use hacer falta in the same way.

Me hace falta un plato.

I need a plate.

Me hacen falta sábanas limpias.

I need some clean sheets.

Quiero un reembolso.

I want a refund.

Quiero cambiar de habitación.

I want to change rooms.

Worked example

READING

Read the text about restaurants.

Los problemas de servicio al cliente

¡Comida fría!

Hay muchos problemas que uno se puede encontrar en un restaurante, pero lo que realmente puede llegar a irritar a un cliente es cuando la comida llega fría. Es una señal clara de que el camarero no está haciendo bien su trabajo.

¡Camareros perdidos!

Otro problema que puede hacer que la experiencia en un restaurante no sea tan buena, es cuando necesitas al camarero y no le puedes encontrar por ninguna parte. Quieres pedir la comida o más bebidas y nunca está cerca de tu mesa. Los buenos camareros siempre están pendientes de sus clientes y de lo que necesitan.

¡Platos sucios!

Platos, cuchillos, tenedores y en definitiva, un restaurante sucio, es terrible siempre. Los camareros deberían limpiar las mesas con regularidad y asegurarse de que todo lo que pongan en la mesa está bien limpio. ¡Nadie se quiere encontrar una mosca en la sopa!

When do customers get annoyed?

A	if the waiter is rude or unfriendly
B	if they have to wait for their bill
C	if their meal is not hot

Write the correct letter in the box. ☐ C   **(1 mark)**

Exam alert

Multiple-choice questions with three options (A, B, C) are used in both listening and reading papers. Do not choose an answer just because you have spotted one word that matches what is in the text; all three options may contain words that feature in the text, but only one is right.

Now try this

READING

Read the text again in the worked example and answer these questions **in English**.

(a) What does food arriving cold at the table tell the customer?   **(1 mark)**

(b) What should waiters do regularly?   **(1 mark)**

Asking for help abroad

You need to be able to ask for help if you run into trouble while abroad.

Ayuda en el extranjero

Necesito ayuda.   I need help.

El coche ha tenido una avería.
The car has broken down.

Quiero denunciar el robo de ...
I want to report the theft of ...

El ladrón era bajo y llevaba gafas.
The thief was short and wore glasses.

No sufrí ningún daño personal.
I did not suffer any physical injury.

Tomó lugar en la estación de servicio.
It took place in the petrol station.

¿Puede darme una ficha oficial?
Can you give me an official form?

No sé dónde está el billetero.
I don't know where my wallet is.

Ayuda en la oficina de objetos perdidos

He perdido ...	I have lost ...
un anillo	a ring
un bolso	a bag
un collar	a necklace
unas gafas de sol	some sunglasses
unas llaves	some keys
un ordenador portátil	a laptop
un paraguas	an umbrella
unos pendientes	some earrings
una pulsera	a bracelet
un sombrero	a hat

Worked example

You have lost something and are in a lost property office in Valencia.
The teacher will play the role of the lost property officer and will speak first.
Estás en la oficina de objetos perdidos de Valencia (España). Has perdido algo.

1 Objeto – descripción
   ¿En qué puedo servirle?
   He perdido mi paraguas. Es azul y pequeño.

2 En Valencia – razón
   ¿Qué hace aquí en España?
   Estoy de vacaciones en Valencia con mi familia.

3 !
   ¿Dónde y cuándo lo ha perdido?
   Lo perdí ayer en el museo.
   Lo siento, pero aquí no está.

4 ? Volver (día) – oficina
   ¿Cuándo puede volver otra vez?
   A lo mejor el lunes.

5 ? Horario – oficina
   ¿Cuál es el horario de la oficina?
   Abrimos a las diez y cerramos a las siete y media.

Exam alert

This is a higher tier role play: it has five prompts and one unprepared question, and you have to ask a question. You are expected to use different tenses in your answers.

Revise question words to help you create questions for the role play task.
¿Qué? What?
¿Cómo? How? What?
¿Dónde? Where?
¿Cuándo? When?
¿A qué hora? At what time?
¿Con quién? With whom?

Now try this

Listen to the recording

Use the vocabulary on this page to help you create your answers.

Imagine you have had your purse stolen in a café. How would you answer these role play questions? Prepare your answers, then listen to the recording and fill in the pauses with your answers. Listen to one student's answers in the Answers section.

1   ¿Qué ha ocurrido exactamente?

2   ¿Dónde ha tenido lugar el robo?

3   ¿Puede describir al ladrón / a la ladrona?

4   ¿Cómo es su monedero?

School subjects

You need to be able to say what subjects you study, what you think of them and why.

Las asignaturas

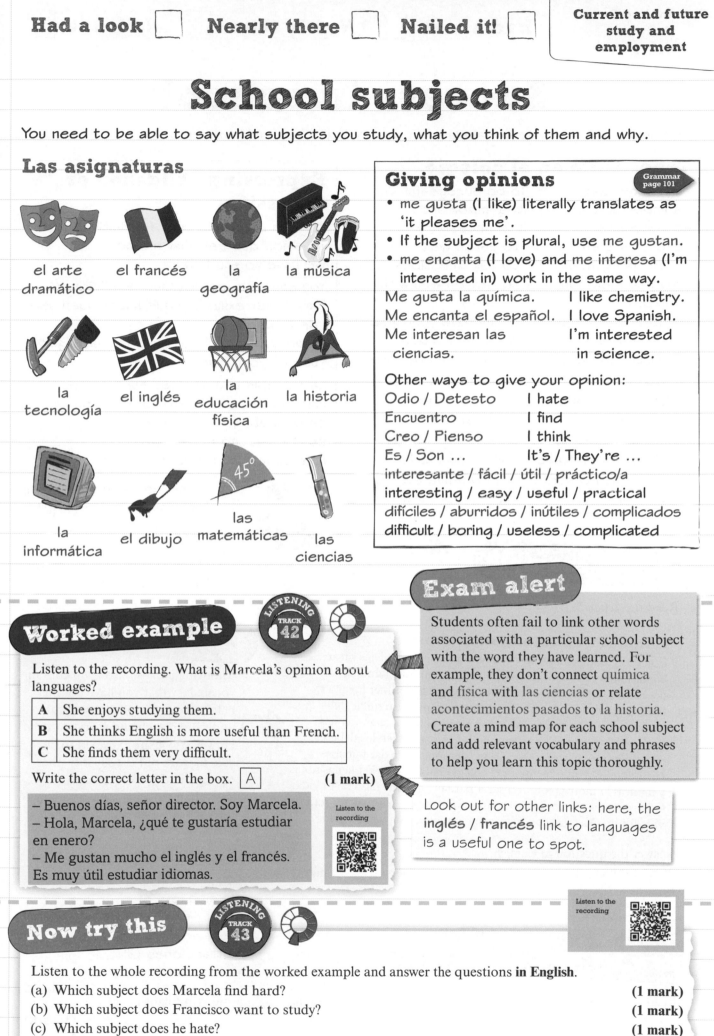

el arte dramático

el francés

la geografía

la música

la tecnología

el inglés

la educación física

la historia

la informática

el dibujo

las matemáticas

las ciencias

Giving opinions
Grammar page 101

- me gusta (I like) literally translates as 'it pleases me'.
- If the subject is plural, use me gustan.
- me encanta (I love) and me interesa (I'm interested in) work in the same way.

Me gusta la química.	I like chemistry.
Me encanta el español.	I love Spanish.
Me interesan las ciencias.	I'm interested in science.

Other ways to give your opinion:

Odio / Detesto	I hate
Encuentro	I find
Creo / Pienso	I think
Es / Son ...	It's / They're ...

interesante / fácil / útil / práctico/a
interesting / easy / useful / practical

difíciles / aburridos / inútiles / complicados
difficult / boring / useless / complicated

Worked example
LISTENING TRACK 42

Listen to the recording. What is Marcela's opinion about languages?

A	She enjoys studying them.
B	She thinks English is more useful than French.
C	She finds them very difficult.

Write the correct letter in the box. ☐ A   **(1 mark)**

– Buenos días, señor director. Soy Marcela.
– Hola, Marcela, ¿qué te gustaría estudiar en enero?
– Me gustan mucho el inglés y el francés. Es muy útil estudiar idiomas.

Listen to the recording

Exam alert

Students often fail to link other words associated with a particular school subject with the word they have learned. For example, they don't connect química and física with las ciencias or relate acontecimientos pasados to la historia. Create a mind map for each school subject and add relevant vocabulary and phrases to help you learn this topic thoroughly.

Look out for other links: here, the inglés / francés link to languages is a useful one to spot.

Now try this
LISTENING TRACK 43

Listen to the recording

Listen to the whole recording from the worked example and answer the questions **in English**.

(a) Which subject does Marcela find hard?   **(1 mark)**

(b) Which subject does Francisco want to study?   **(1 mark)**

(c) Which subject does he hate?   **(1 mark)**

(d) What does he think of art?   **(1 mark)**

Success in school

Use this page to revise vocabulary for describing school achievements.

Tener éxito en el colegio

Para tener éxito …	To be successful …
es importante …	it is important …
es necesario …	it is necessary …
escuchar bien	to listen well
hacer preguntas	to ask questions
llevarte bien con otros	to get on well with others
mejorar tus notas	to improve your grades
estar motivado/a	to be motivated
organizar tu tiempo	to organise your time
aprovechar las oportunidades	to take advantage of opportunities
dormir bien	to sleep well
desarrollar buenos hábitos de estudio	to develop good studying habits
no dejar todo para el último momento	not to leave everything to the last minute

Expressing obligation or necessity

You can use tener que + infinitive:
Tenemos que estudiar mucho.
We have to study a lot.

You can also use hay que + infinitive:
Para tener éxito hay que hacer buen uso de tu agenda.
To be successful you have to make good use of your planner/diary.

Or you can use phrases such as es importante, es necesario, es esencial, es obligatorio + infinitive:
Es esencial no perder tiempo.
It is essential not to waste time.

Es necesario encontrar un lugar cómodo y tranquilo para hacer los deberes.
You have to find a comfortable and quiet place to do your homework.

Worked example

 READING

Read the article.

Cómo ser un estudiante exitoso

Ir al colegio todos los días es muy importante si quieres sacar buenas notas, pero hay otro tipo de atributos que también son necesarios para ser un estudiante de éxito. En primer lugar, es fundamental evitar las distracciones. Esto puede resultar difícil pero es muy importante. Apaga siempre el móvil cuando estés haciendo los deberes. En segundo lugar, hacer bien los deberes en casa y prestar atención en clase siempre van a dar buenos resultados. Cuando termines el colegio habrás sacado buenas notas y tendrás la motivación necesaria para el siguiente paso de tu vida. Cuanto antes te conviertas en un estudiante de éxito, mejor será tu vida futura. Vas a necesitar paciencia, motivación y tenacidad.

Answer the question **in English**.
What is difficult to manage but essential for success?   **(1 mark)**
Avoiding distractions

In this text, although there are complex constructions, there are also lots of cognates which help you decode the passage: **atributos** (attributes), **distracciones** (distractions), **motivación** (motivation), etc.

Now try this

 READING

Read the article in the worked example again and answer the following questions **in English**.

(a) How can you avoid distractions at home?   **(1 mark)**

(b) What **two** things always lead to good results?   **(2 marks)**

(c) What characteristics will you have to possess? Name **one**.   **(1 mark)**

School life

Use the vocabulary on this page to talk about your life in school.

La vida en el instituto

Presto atención en clase.	I pay attention in class.
Llevo mi bloc de notas.	I bring my pad of paper.
Repaso las asignaturas.	I revise my subjects.
Hago exámenes.	I do exams.
Escribo ensayos.	I write essays.
Corrijo los ejercicios.	I correct my exercises.
Contesto las preguntas de los profesores.	I answer the teachers.
Hablo con mis compañeros.	I talk to my classmates.
Saludo al conserje.	I greet the caretaker.
A veces me castigan.	I sometimes get detention.
No suspendo las pruebas.	I don't fail my tests.
Queremos aprobar el examen final.	We want to pass the final exam.
Voy al club de ciencias.	I go to science club.
Hacemos experimentos.	We do experiments.

Negatives

Grammar page 100

No (not) goes before the verb:
No voy al club de ajedrez.
I don't go to chess club.
Los pasillos no están muy llenos.
The corridors are not very busy.

Other negatives go after a verb with no before it, or before the verb:
No copio nunca de la pizarra.
I never copy from the board.
Nunca usamos libros de texto.
We never use textbooks.
No hay nadie en la sala de profesores.
There is no one in the staff room.
Nadie repitió el curso.
No one repeated the year.
No … ni … means 'not (either) … or …'
No estudio sociología ni periodismo.
I don't study sociology or media studies.

Worked example

Traduce las frases siguientes **al español**.

(a) I always do my homework. **(2 marks)**
   Siempre hago mis deberes.

(b) I talk with my classmates during break. **(2 marks)**
   Hablo con mis compañeros durante el recreo.

(c) Last week I worked hard in maths. **(3 marks)**
   La semana pasada trabajé duro en matemáticas.

(d) I don't like revising my subjects but it's important. **(3 marks)**

   No me gusta repasar mis materias pero es importante.

Exam alert

When translating into Spanish, you will be marked on accuracy and communication. To answer successfully, you need to check that your verbs are in the correct tense and have the correct person ending.

All the verbs are in the correct tenses and use the correct endings: **hago, hablo, trabajé, no me gusta repasar, es.** Make sure your other vocabulary is accurate, too: in **la semana pasada, pasada** ends in -a because **semana** is a feminine noun.

Now try this

Traduce las frases siguientes **al español**.

(a) I never talk to my friends in class. **(2 marks)**
(b) I sometimes read books in the library. **(2 marks)**
(c) Yesterday morning I wrote a history essay. **(3 marks)**
(d) I prefer talking to the teacher because I hate copying from the board. **(3 marks)**

The school day

Make sure you can describe your school routine.

El día en el instituto

Voy al instituto en tren.
I go to school by train.
Llego a las ocho y cuarto.
I arrive at quarter past eight.
Las clases empiezan a las nueve menos veinte.
Classes start at twenty to nine.
Como algo durante el recreo.
I eat something during break.
El descanso para almorzar dura cincuenta minutos.
The lunch break lasts fifty minutes.
Las clases terminan a las tres y media.
Classes finish at three thirty.
Entreno en el equipo de bádminton del instituto.
I train for the school badminton team.
Después del instituto voy al coro.
After school I go to choir.

¿Qué hora es?

midday = mediodía
midnight = medianoche

en punto

menos cinco — y cinco
menos diez — y diez

12
11 son las doce 1
son las once es las una
10 son las diez — son las dos 2

HORAS

9 son las nueve — MINUTOS — son las tres 3

menos cuarto — y cuarto

son las ocho 8 — son las cuatro 4
son las siete — son las seis — son las cinco
7 6 5

menos veinte — y veinte

menos veinticinco — y veinticinco

y media

a.m. = de la mañana   p.m. = de la tarde / de la noche

Worked example

Read José's text about his school day.

En invierno voy al instituto en autobús porque hace mucho frío. Normalmente llego a las nueve menos veinte y voy directamente al patio para charlar con mis amigos. Las clases empiezan a las nueve y lo malo es que solo tenemos quince minutos de recreo durante la mañana. El descanso para almorzar también es muy corto porque empieza a las doce y termina a la una menos cuarto. Las clases terminan a las tres y cuarto pero siempre hago alguna actividad antes de volver a casa.

Answer the question **in English**.
What does José do first when he gets to school? **(1 mark)**
He goes to chat with his friends in the playground.

Reading strategies

Remember that you are not going to find an exact translation of the information requested by the question. You need to deduce meaning and think about how information can be conveyed in different ways.

Here, you will not find the word 'first', **primero**, in the text. Instead, look for what José describes after his arrival at school: **llego a las nueve menos veinte y …** . The word **directamente** shows that he does not do anything else before going to the playground. If you cannot remember the word **patio**, you could guess where you might talk with your friends before school, ruling out any vocabulary you can remember, such as **clase** or **comedor**.

Now try this

Read the text in the worked example again and answer the following questions **in English**.
(a) What is not good about morning break?   **(1 mark)**
(b) How long does lunch last?   **(1 mark)**
(c) How do you know José does not go home at 3.15pm?   **(1 mark)**

Comparing schools

Be prepared to compare Spanish schools with schools in your own country.

Mi instituto, tu instituto

En España ...	In Spain ...
hay menos exámenes.	there are fewer exams.
no estudian ciertas asignaturas.	they do not study certain subjects.
las vacaciones son más largas.	the holidays are longer.
la jornada escolar es más corta.	the school day is shorter.
no comen en el instituto.	they don't eat lunch at school.
los estudiantes llaman a sus profesores por su nombre.	students call their teachers by their first name.

Los alumnos no tienen que llevar uniforme.
Students do not have to wear uniform.

Aiming higher

Avoid using me gusta and odio all the time – stand out from the crowd by using something more impressive ...

No lo aguanto. I can't stand it.	No lo aguantaba. I couldn't stand it.
No lo soporto. I can't bear it.	No lo soportaba. I couldn't bear it.
No me importa. It's not important to me. / I don't mind.	No me importaba. It was not important to me. / I didn't mind.
Me enoja. / molesta. It annoys me.	Me enojaba. / molestaba. It annoyed me.
No es justo. It's not fair.	No era justo. It wasn't fair.
Me da igual ... I'm not bothered about ...	Me daba igual ... I wasn't bothered about ...

Worked example

 SPEAKING

¿Qué diferencias hay entre los institutos en España y en Inglaterra?

Los colegios en España son diferentes de los colegios ingleses. Los alumnos no llevan uniforme y las clases terminan a las dos. Además, las vacaciones son más largas: casi tres meses. ¡Me gustaría ir al instituto en España!

AIMING HIGHER

En Inglaterra los alumnos llevan uniforme y no lo soporto, pero visité un instituto español durante un intercambio y ¡qué sorpresa! Los alumnos españoles no tenían que llevarlo. ¡Qué envidia! ¡No es justo! Lo que más me gusta es que las vacaciones son más largas y por eso preferiría estar en España.

Aiming higher

Try working in expressions like these:
No es justo que ...
It's not fair that ...
¡Ojalá pudiera tener más vacaciones!
If only I could have more holidays!

- Use of other tenses (**visité**) adds sophistication to this answer.
- **Exclamation phrases** are also useful to show opinions.
- Using more interesting opinions (**¡No es justo!**) makes the language more complex, as does the inclusion of a conditional: **preferiría** (I would prefer).

Now try this

 SPEAKING

 Try to include some different information and express a preference.

Habla de las diferencias entre los institutos en España y en Inglaterra.

Describing schools

Use this page to learn vocabulary for describing your school facilities and activities.

Mi instituto

En la mochila tengo …
In my school bag I have …

un estuche.	a pencil case.
unos lápices.	some pencils.
unas tijeras.	scissors.
un sacapuntas.	a sharpener.
un bolígrafo.	a pen.
(barra de) pegamento.	glue (stick).
unos cuadernos.	some exercise books.

En mi instituto de enseñanza
   secundaria hay …
In my secondary school
   there is/are …

un comedor.	a canteen.
unos vestuarios.	some changing rooms.
muchas aulas.	lots of classrooms.
un gimnasio.	a gymnasium.
un laboratorio de idiomas.	a language lab.
un despacho.	a school office.

No tenemos autobús escolar.
We don't have a school bus.
No hay campo de deportes.
There is no sports field.

Using the verb tener in different tenses

Tener (to have) is a verb you need to know. Be ready to use it in different tenses. It is a radical-changing verb (note the vowel change in the present).

	Present	Preterite	Future
I	tengo	tuve	tendré
you	tienes	tuviste	tendrás
he / she / it	tiene	tuvo	tendrá
we	tenemos	tuvimos	tendremos
you (pl.)	tenéis	tuvisteis	tendréis
they	tienen	tuvieron	tendrás

El año pasado tuvimos que llevar una calculadora a todas las clases de matemáticas.
Last year we had to bring a calculator to all our maths lessons.

Worked example

Describe tu instituto. Menciona:
- cómo es
- tu opinión
- las instalaciones
- algunos cambios recientes.

(16 marks)

No me gusta mucho mi instituto, es muy viejo y bastante pequeño. No hay biblioteca y hay pocos ordenadores, así que es difícil hacer los deberes. Construyeron una piscina el año pasado. Desafortunadamente no me gusta nada nadar.

This student has done well to include opinions as well as introducing the **preterite tense** but a greater **variety** of vocabulary and tenses would be needed for a higher-level answer.

AIMING HIGHER Mi instituto es grande y moderno y tiene muchas instalaciones, por eso me gusta mucho. No tenemos muchas instalaciones deportivas, así que van a construir una nueva pista de atletismo. Tenemos también aulas nuevas porque el año pasado se construyeron nuevos edificios.

This answer includes more detail. Using a passive form like **se construyeron** also shows that you know, and can use, a wider range of structures accurately.

Now try this

Write your own answer to the writing task in the worked example. Write approximately **90** words.   **(16 marks)**

School rules

This page will help you talk about school rules and what you think of them.

Las normas del instituto

En mi instituto …	In my school …
No se puede …	You can't …
Está prohibido …	It is forbidden to …
No se debe …	You mustn't …
llevar maquillaje.	wear make-up.
usar el MP3 en clase.	use your MP3 in class.
comer chicle.	chew gum.
usar el móvil.	use your mobile.
mandar mensajes.	send messages.
llegar tarde.	arrive late.
correr en/por los pasillos.	run in the corridors.
ser antipático.	be unpleasant.
hablar mientras habla el profesor.	talk while the teacher is talking.

No se debe ser ni desobediente ni grosero.

You mustn't be either disobedient or rude.

Son tontas / necesarias / anticuadas / útiles / inútiles.

They are stupid / necessary / old fashioned / useful / useless.

Key verbs + the infinitive

	querer – to want	poder – be able to	deber – to have to, must
I	quiero	puedo	debo
you	quieres	puedes	debes
he / she / it	quiere	puede	debe
we	queremos	podemos	debemos
you	queréis	podéis	debéis
they	quieren	pueden	deben

Quiere llevar pendientes pero no se puede llevar joyas.
She wants to wear earrings but you can't wear jewellery.

Worked example 🗣 SPEAKING

¿Existen normas en tu instituto?

En mi instituto tengo que llevar uniforme. Odio el uniforme porque es incómodo. En mi opinión, las normas son anticuadas. Son tontas e inútiles pero algunas personas piensan que son necesarias. ¡Qué horror!

Use a variety of opinion words and adjectives (**incómodo, anticuadas, inútiles**) to say not only what you think, but also what others think – this will help you to aim for a higher grade.

AIMING HIGHER

En mi instituto, hay muchas normas. Acaban de introducir una nueva y ahora no se permite usar el móvil en clase. ¡No es justo! Hay que dejarlo en casa, o apagarlo antes de entrar en el instituto. Creo que los profesores son demasiado estrictos.

Use idiomatic phrases such as **acaban de**. They add variety to your language and make it sound more sophisticated. Try adding an exclamation phrase as well (**¡No es justo!**).

Now try this 🗣 SPEAKING

Answer this question. Speak for about one minute.

• ¿Existen normas en tu instituto?

Try to include:
• three opinions / adjectives
• three connectives
• three different phrases with the infinitive
• a Spanish exclamation.

Problems at school

Use this page to talk about the pressures and problems you face at school.

Los problemas en el instituto

Tienes que ...	You have to ...
respetar a todo el mundo.	respect everyone.
sacar buenas notas.	get good grades.
aprobar los exámenes.	pass exams.
tener buenas calificaciones.	have good qualifications.
mejorar tu rendimiento.	improve your performance.
pensar en el futuro.	think about the future.

No se debería ...	You should not ...
acosar / intimidar.	bully.
reñir.	quarrel.
pelear.	fight.
molestar.	annoy.
hacer novillos.	bunk lessons.
Hay mucha presión.	There is a lot of pressure (to achieve good marks).
el boletín de notas	school report
la vuelta al instituto	the first day back at school

The preposition 'a'

When the direct object of a verb is a person, you add a before the person. This is not translated into English.

Miguel intimida a otros alumnos.
Miguel intimidates other pupils.

No se debería insultar a los demás.
You should not insult other people.

el acoso escolar	bullying
estresante	stressful
débil	weak
torpe	clumsy
grosero	rude

Worked example

LISTENING TRACK 44

Listen to the start of a conversation about problems at school. What problem is mentioned? **(1 mark)**

A bullying
B pressure to do well
C no free time
D messy environment
E timetable problems
F journey to school
G fighting in the playground

Write the correct letter in the first box. `B` ☐ ☐

Listen to the recording

– Yo tengo miedo de no aprobar los exámenes. Mis padres esperan mucho de mí.

Exam alert

Avoid common errors such as just listening for one or two specific words. Think about all possible words that may be applicable for each category. So for bullying, don't just focus on acoso but listen for intimidar (to intimidate), insultar (to insult), molestar (to annoy), pelearse (to fight), una pelea (a fight), etc.

In this question you do not hear the word **presión**, but instead the pressure is explained with **tengo miedo de no aprobar** (I am afraid of not passing) and **mis padres esperan mucho de mí** (my parents expect a lot from me).

Now try this

LISTENING TRACK 45

Look at the worked example. Listen to the rest of the conversation and write the correct letters in the other two boxes. **(2 marks)**

Listen to the recording

Primary school

Use the imperfect tense to describe what you did at primary school.

La escuela primaria

Cuando tenía diez años era travieso.
When I was 10, I was naughty.
Iba a una escuela de primaria cerca de mi casa.
I used to go to a primary school near my house.
Tenía menos amigos.
I used to have fewer friends.
Jugaba solamente con mis amigas.
I only used to play with my female friends.
Comía los bocadillos que mi madre me preparaba.
I used to eat sandwiches that my mother prepared.
No estudiaba español.   I didn't study Spanish.

Hacía más deporte.
I used to do more sport.

The imperfect tense

 Grammar page 94

The imperfect tense is used to describe what **used to happen** or what **was happening**.
It is formed as follows:

hablar to speak	comer to eat	vivir to live
hablaba	comía	vivía
hablabas	comías	vivías
hablaba	comía	vivía
hablábamos	comíamos	vivíamos
hablabais	comíais	vivíais
hablaban	comían	vivían

Exam strategies

Learn tenses by chanting them – hablaba, hablabas, hablaba ... Start off by reading them, then close your book and see how many you can chant without looking. Keep going until you can do the whole verb.

Worked example

WRITING

Escribe sobre tu vida escolar. Menciona:
• tus experiencias de la escuela primaria.   **(16 marks)**

AIMING HIGHER Cuando tenía diez años era travieso y la escuela primaria era aburrida. Estudiaba muchas asignaturas y muchos idiomas. La lengua que más me gustaba era el francés. Durante el recreo, salíamos al patio y jugábamos a juegos muy animados y ruidosos como el fútbol. También corríamos carreras. Teníamos mucha energía. De pequeño, estaba más contento porque tenía más amigos. La vida era más fácil, no tenía tantos deberes y los profesores eran menos severos.

Exam alert

Make sure that your writing is clear and legible. You will not be successful if the examiner cannot read your writing and therefore cannot grade your communication or accuracy.

Aiming higher

☑ Including **imperfect** tense verbs shows a confident and secure use of a tense.
☑ Use a **variety** of vocabulary (here, idiomas / lengua).
☑ An **opinion** phrase in the imperfect (me gustaba) is always a good addition.

Now try this

WRITING

Escribe sobre tus experiencias de la escuela primaria. Escribe aproximadamente **75 palabras en español**. **(16 marks)**

School trips

Revise vocabulary and structures to help you describe your school trips.

Una excursión del colegio

Fuimos a ...   We went to ...

durante las vacaciones de mitad de trimestre
during half term

Practicamos el español / francés / italiano.
We practised Spanish / French / Italian.

Nuestro profesor de español nos acompañó.
Our Spanish teacher accompanied us.

Aprendimos mucho.   We learned a lot.

Disfrutamos de un día especial.
We enjoyed a special day.

Visitamos el museo.   We visited the museum.

Conocimos el parque.   We got to know the park.

Hicimos unas actividades culturales.
We did some cultural activities.

Fue una experiencia divertida.
It was an enjoyable experience.

Using a variety of tenses

✓ You can say what you **normally** do on trips:
Normalmente vamos a un museo.
Normally we go to a museum.

✓ Say what you did **on a recent trip**:
Fuimos al cine para ver una película española.
We went to the cinema to see a Spanish film.

✓ Say what you **used to** do on past trips:
En la escuela primaria las excursiones eran más cortas.
In primary school trips used to be shorter.

✓ Say what you **will** do for your next trip:
Aprenderemos mucho español.
We will learn a lot of Spanish.

Worked example

Read the article.
Why do children love school trips?

A	They don't have to get up early.
B	They love being with their friends.
C	They feel as if it is a day off from their studies.

Write the correct letter in the box. [C]   **(1 mark)**

Don't worry if there is a lot of unfamiliar vocabulary! If you know some of this topic vocabulary, you can work out that the answer is C from **no tienen que ir al colegio**.

Las excursiones escolares

A los niños les encantan las excursiones porque no tienen que ir al colegio, sentarse en clase a leer y escribir o escuchar a la profesora durante horas. Nosotros los profesores sabemos que llevar a los niños de excursión tiene muchas ventajas. En las excursiones los niños conocen lugares nuevos y también aprenden a relacionarse entre sí de una manera más positiva: mientras van en el autobús o durante la hora de la comida. Es posible que hasta hablen con niños que no forman parte de su grupo habitual de amigos. Algunos niños nunca han visitado museos, entrado dentro de una biblioteca o visto los animales de una granja o en un zoo. Lo mejor de las excursiones es que muchos niños visitan lugares a los que sus padres no les llevarían normalmente y esto es enriquecedor porque expande sus mentes y les permite entrar en contacto con mundos y realidades distintas.

Now try this

Read the article in the worked example again. Write the correct letter in each box.

(a) The benefits of trips are ...   **A** clear to teachers   **B** surprising   **C** not educational   ☐ **(1 mark)**

(b) The text does not mention a trip to a ...   **A** museum   **B** farm   **C** church   ☐ **(1 mark)**

(c) For some children, a trip will be ...   **A** too expensive   **B** tiring   **C** a new experience   ☐ **(1 mark)**

School events

Revise vocabulary for describing events that take place at your school.

Los eventos en el instituto

un concurso de talentos   a talent show
un campeonato de remo
a rowing championship
muchos torneos de fútbol
lots of football tournaments
un partido de balonmano
a handball match
una obra de teatro   a play
un concierto de la orquesta del instituto
a school orchestra concert
la fiesta de fin de curso   the-end-of-year party
una reunión con el orientador
a meeting with the careers adviser

Recaudamos fondos para nuestra área de recreo.
We are fundraising for our playground.

Desde hace and desde

Use desde hace ('for') to say how long you have been doing something. It is used with the **present** tense of the verb.

Canto en el coro desde hace dos años.
I have been singing in the choir for two years.

Nuestro instituto participa en el concurso de ortografía desde hace cinco años.
Our school has been taking part in the spelling competition for five years.

Use desde ('since') to say when you started doing something. It is also used with the **present** tense of the verb.

Entrenamos para el partido desde marzo.
We have been training for the match since March.

Worked example

 LISTENING TRACK 46

Listen to the head teacher's speech and answer the question **in English**.
Why was it such a successful year for school sport? Give **two** reasons.   (2 marks)

Listen to the recording

basketball team won eight out of ten matches / school won five gold karate medals

– El equipo de baloncesto ha ganado ocho de los últimos diez partidos y los participantes en el campeonato regional de kárate han vuelto con cinco medallas de oro.

Exam alert

Pay attention to the number of marks available. Where there are two marks, you will need to give two pieces of information. The instruction will always be highlighted in bold where this is required, so make sure you read the instructions carefully.

To answer this question successfully, you need to identify the activity and **also** what they won. Therefore you need to pick out numbers too: ocho de los últimos diez and cinco medallas de oro.

Now try this

 LISTENING TRACK 47

Listen to the recording

Listen to the rest of the speech from the worked example and answer the following questions **in English**.
(a) What other achievement is mentioned in the speech?   (1 mark)
(b) Which event does the head teacher mention as being her favourite?   (1 mark)
(c) Who does she congratulate?   (1 mark)

School exchanges

Use this page to learn how to talk about exchange visits.

Los intercambios

Nos ayudan a ...   They help us to ...
Te permiten ...   They allow you to ...
  viajar a / conocer otro país
  travel to / get to know another country
  aprender de otras culturas y costumbres
  learn about other cultures and customs
  entender más fácilmente / dominar otros
   idiomas
  understand other languages more easily /
   speak other languages well
  vivir una gran aventura
  experience a great adventure
  experimentar algo nuevo
  experience something new
Tienen beneficios incalculables para tu futuro.
They have invaluable benefits for your future.

¿Qué hiciste?

Estuve con una familia.   I stayed with a family.
Hice nuevos amigos.   I made new friends.
Fui a clase de distintas asignaturas.
I attended different lessons.
Vi el mundo de forma diferente.
I saw the world differently.
Hice varias actividades culturales.
I did some cultural activities.
Fui a dos excursiones.
I went on two trips.
El intercambio duró una semana.
The exchange lasted a week.
Creé entradas en el blog del intercambio.
I wrote entries for the exchange blog.

Comí platos típicos.
I ate typical dishes.

Worked example

 SPEAKING

Topic: Cultural life
Prepare your answers to the bullet points.
1 ¿Qué hay en la foto?
En esta foto hay un grupo de
estudiantes ingleses que hacen un
intercambio en España. Han visitado el
centro histórico de la ciudad.

2 ¿Qué piensas de los intercambios?
A mí me encantan los intercambios porque te permiten
hacer nuevos amigos de otro país.

3 Describe un intercambio o una excursión cultural de tu instituto.
El año pasado estuve con una familia muy amable de
Madrid. Aprendí mucho español y fue muy interesante ir al
instituto.

4 ?
En el futuro me gustaría ir a Sudamérica. Quiero aprender
más de la cultura latinoamericana.

5 ?
Los intercambios son importantes porque nos ayudan a
conocer otros países y a dominar otros idiomas.

Exam alert

In the picture-based discussion,
the examiner will ask you the three
questions as they appear on the card.
You then have to answer two more
questions that you have not prepared.

The examiner's questions
would be:
**4. ¿Adónde te gustaría ir
y por qué?**
**5. ¿Por qué son
importantes los
intercambios?**
This candidate uses a
range of tenses and some
complex vocabulary to
answer each point.

Now try this

 SPEAKING TRACK 48   Listen to the recording

Prepare your own answers to the picture-based questions in the worked example above. Then listen to the
track and speak your answers in the pauses. Listen to one student's answers in the Answers section.

Future plans

Using the future tense and the subjunctive to talk about future plans will make your writing and speaking more natural.

Tus planes para el futuro

Cuando sea mayor ...	When I'm older ...
Cuando termine la universidad ...	When I finish university ...
Trabajaré como ...	I'll work as ...
Trabajaré en el extranjero.	I'll work abroad.
Seré rico/a.	I'll be rich.
Ganaré la lotería.	I'll win the lottery.
Viajaré mucho.	I'll travel a lot.
Seré famoso/a.	I'll be famous.
Ganaré mucho dinero.	I'll earn lots of money.
Seré muy feliz.	I will be very happy.
Me casaré y tendré hijos.	I'll get married and have children.
Es un campo en el que me gustaría trabajar.	It's a field in which I would like to work.

The subjunctive

Grammar page 99

The subjunctive is used after cuando to talk about an event in the future. To form the subjunctive, replace the infinitive ending with the following:

hablar to speak	comer to eat	vivir to live
hable	coma	viva
hables	comas	vivas
hable	coma	viva
hablemos	comamos	vivamos
habléis	comáis	viváis
hablen	coman	vivan

Cuando tenga veinte años, viajaré mucho. When I'm 20, I'll travel a lot.

Worked example

* ¿Cuáles son tus planes para el futuro?

  No sé qué voy a hacer después de los exámenes. Me gustaría trabajar en el extranjero porque me encanta visitar nuevos lugares.

AIMING HIGHER Cuando sea mayor y termine la universidad, viajaré mucho. Ganaré mucho dinero, así que seré feliz porque podré comprar mucha ropa.

* Use the future tense (viajaré, ganaré) to say what you will do.
* Use connectives (así que, porque) to justify your opinions and to create more impressive sentences.
* There is a good example of how to use cuando + the subjunctive to add variety to what you say.

Now try this

Answer this question. Speak for about one minute.
* ¿Cuáles son tus planes para el futuro?

Try to include:
* one or two subjunctive phrases
* two or three future tense phrases
* an opinion phrase.

Future education plans

Use ir with the infinitive to talk about what you're going to do when you finish school.

Qué hacer en el futuro

el año que viene / el año próximo	next year
en el futuro	in the future
No estoy seguro/a.	I'm not sure.
Si saco buenas notas ...	If I get good grades ...
Voy a ...	I'm going to ...
estudiar lenguas / idiomas	study languages
ir a la universidad	go to university
buscar / encontrar empleo	look for / find a job
tomar un año libre / sabático	take a gap year
tener éxito	be successful

seguir estudiando en el instituto
continue studying in my school

ir a otro instituto para alumnos de 16 a 18 años
go to a sixth-form college

ganar mucho dinero
earn lots of money

Immediate future tense

This form of the future (using ir + infinitive) is like the English 'going to', and is used to express plans and intentions.

Grammar page 95

I	voy		ir
you	vas		buscar
he / she / it	va		hacer
we	vamos	a	seguir
you	vais		trabajar
they	van		estudiar

Voy a ir a la universidad.
I'm going to go to university.
Va a estudiar música.
He is going to study music.

Worked example

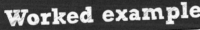 

Escribe un texto sobre tu instituto. Menciona:
• Tus planes para el futuro.

El año que viene voy a estudiar idiomas porque me encanta el español y es fácil e interesante.

 Quiero seguir estudiando el año próximo. Me gustaría estudiar idiomas porque me encanta saber más de otras culturas. Es más, el año pasado saqué buenas notas en español. Si sigo sacando buenas notas en el futuro, iré a la universidad porque quiero ser traductora en la Unión Europea.

Aiming higher

✓ **Vary** your tenses – this makes your answer more interesting and lets you show off what you know.

✓ **Develop** your answer – always look for opportunities to add more information, e.g. Es más, el año pasado saqué buenas notas ... What's more, last year I got good marks.

✓ Make it **stand out** – an unusual twist will help distinguish it, e.g. quiero ser traductora en la Unión Europea. I want to be a translator in the European Union.

✓ **Impress** with interesting structures: Si sigo sacando buenas notas en el futuro, iré ... If I keep getting good grades in the future, I will go ... .

Now try this

Write about your future plans. Write at least **30–40** words **in Spanish**.

(8 marks)

Using languages

Use this page to help you talk about the importance of learning another language.

Los idiomas

Vivimos en una sociedad global.
We live in a global society.
Aprender otro idioma es importante porque puedes …
Learning another language is important because you can …

mejorar tu carrera.	improve your career.
conseguir un trabajo más fácilmente.	find a job more easily.
obtener un mejor salario.	get a better salary.
trabajar como traductor(a).	work as a translator.
disfrutar mejor de tus viajes.	enjoy your trips more.
comunicarte mejor en otros países.	communicate better in other countries.
entender más del mundo.	understand more about the world.
conocer más gente.	get to know more people.
mejorar tu memoria.	improve your memory.

Aiming higher

Learn as many verbs as you can. They will help elevate your language and make it easier to express more abstract ideas. Make your own list of exciting verbs that can be used across different topic areas. For each verb, write an example for the first person (yo) in a different tense. Watch out for the irregular verbs!

Infinitive	mejorar (reg) to improve	obtener (irreg) to obtain
Preterite	mejoré	obtuve
Present	mejoro	obtengo
Near future	voy a mejorar	voy a obtener
Future	mejoraré	obtendré

Worked example

READING

Read the article.
Answer the question **in English**.
Where is Spanish the official language?   **(1 mark)**

in more than 20 countries

You will not find a long list of countries in the text, but instead a sentence which says where you can travel with Spanish: **se habla en más de 20 países.**

¿Por qué estudiar español?

Hoy en día es necesario aprender un segundo idioma. Aprender español es tanto útil como divertido. ¿Por qué? Hay varias razones de peso:

- El español es muy útil a la hora de viajar, se habla en más de 20 países donde es la lengua oficial.
- El español es un idioma clave para los negocios en EEUU y en muchas partes del mundo.
- Aprender otra lengua, como el español, te puede ayudar a conocer mejor tu propio idioma y además te puede facilitar aprender otros idiomas distintos.

Y por si todavía necesitas encontrar razones para aprender el español: según un estudio del Instituto Cervantes, más de 500 millones de personas hablan español, esto representa más del 6% de la población mundial. Además, después del chino, el español es el segundo idioma mas hablado del mundo y el segundo más utilizado después del inglés. Se cree que para el año 2030 el 7,5% de la población mundial hablará español.

Now try this

READING

Read the article again from the worked example and answer these questions **in English**.

(a) Give **two** reasons why learning Spanish is useful.   **(2 marks)**

(b) What do six per cent of the world's population do?   **(1 mark)**

(c) Which language is most widely spoken in the world?   **(1 mark)**

(d) Spanish is becoming more popular. How do you know this?   **(1 mark)**

Jobs

Use this page to help you talk about the different jobs people do.

Empleos

un abogado	a lawyer
un actor	an actor
un agente de policía / un policía	a police officer
un agricultor	a farmer
un auxiliar de vuelo / una azafata	an airline steward / stewardess
un arquitecto	an architect
un bombero	a firefighter
un cajero	a cashier
un camarero	a waiter
un cocinero	a cook
un albañil	a builder
un dentista	a dentist
un enfermero	a nurse
un fontanero	a plumber
un funcionario	a civil servant
un informático	a computer scientist
un ingeniero	an engineer
un médico	a doctor
un panadero	a baker
un periodista	a journalist
estar en paro	to be unemployed
el desempleo	unemployment

Using ser to say what jobs people do

Use the verb ser to say what jobs people do. Leave out the indefinite article:

Soy cocinero.   I'm a cook.
Es modelo.   She's a model.
Es camarero.   He's a waiter.

Feminine forms

If the job is done by a woman, change -o to -a and add -a to the ending -or:

cocinero ➡ cocinera   camarero ➡ camarera
agricultor ➡ agricultora

Note some exceptions: actor ➡ actriz
Some jobs are the same in the masculine and feminine: periodista, dentista

Trabajar in different tenses

Present	Imperfect	Future
trabajo I work	trabajaba I used to work	trabajaré I will work

---

Worked example

LISTENING TRACK 49

Listen and answer the question **in English**.
How old is Paco? 30   **(1 mark)**

Listen to the recording

– Hola. Me llamo Paco y tengo treinta años.

Listening strategies

✓ You'll hear every recording **twice**, so don't worry if you don't catch all the answers on first listening.

✓ Keep pace with the recording: if you've missed an answer, go on to the next question.

✓ Don't simply write down the first relevant item of vocabulary you hear. Make sure you listen to the **end** of a recording before you make your final decision.

Now try this

LISTENING TRACK 50

Listen to the recording

Listen to the whole recording from the worked example and answer the questions **in English**.

(a) Which job did Paco use to do?   **(1 mark)**
(b) Why did Paco stop doing that job?   **(1 mark)**
(c) What does he do now?   **(1 mark)**
(d) What job will he do in the future? **(1 mark)**
(e) Why does he want to do this job?   **(1 mark)**

Opinions about jobs

Be ready to understand and give a range of opinions on jobs – both positive and negative.

Opiniones sobre empleos 😀

Me gusta tener responsabilidades.	I like having responsibility.
Me encanta trabajar en contacto con la gente.	I love having contact with people.
Me gusta la variedad.	I like variety.
Me encanta trabajar en equipo.	I love working in a team.
Me gusta la flexibilidad.	I like flexibility.
Está bien pagado.	It's well paid.

Opiniones sobre empleos 🙁

Es un trabajo difícil.	It's a difficult job.
Odio trabajar solo.	I hate working alone.
No me gustan los clientes maleducados.	I don't like rude customers.
Está mal pagado.	It's badly paid.
Odio al jefe.	I hate the boss.
Trabajo muchas horas.	I work long hours.
Estoy de pie todo el día.	I'm on my feet all day.

Me gusta ayudar a la gente.
I like helping people.

Es aburrido y monótono.
It's boring and repetitive.

Worked example

 READING

Read the text.

> Trabajo en una comisaría y me encanta la responsabilidad que tengo. No gano mucho dinero porque el sueldo es bajo. Trabajo muchas horas, sobre todo el sábado y el domingo, pero trabajar los fines de semana me divierte más por la variedad de casos que hay.

What is Paco's job?

A	postman
B	policeman
C	fireman

Write the correct letter in the box. [B]   **(1 mark)**

Exam alert

Make sure that you do not become distracted by the other options supplied in a multiple-choice question. Often you will find all the options in the text, but you must read carefully to work out the correct answer.

Knowing the places people work helps you make the link to their job: una **comisaría** **a police station**

It is important to learn little words like **mucho** (a lot) or **poco** (a little) as they can change the meaning quite radically. In this text, Paco says he does not earn much money, so you can rule out 'salary' as the answer to (a).

Now try this

 READING

Read the text in the worked example again and write the correct letter in each box.

(a) What does Paco like about his job?

A	the hours
B	the salary
C	the responsibility

☐   **(1 mark)**

(b) How does Paco find the work at the weekend?

A	boring
B	varied
C	quiet

☐   **(1 mark)**

Applying for jobs

Use this page to prepare for exam questions concerning job applications and interviews.

Solicitar trabajo

una oferta de trabajo — a job advert

Muy señor mío — Dear Sir

Me dirijo a usted para solicitar el puesto de …
I am writing to apply for the post of …

Le adjunto mi currículum. — I attach my CV.

Domino perfectamente el alemán.
I am a fluent German speaker.

Tengo varias habilidades. — I have various skills.

He rellenado la solicitud.
I have filled in the application form.

Me he formado como aprendiz en …
I have done an apprenticeship in …

Quedo a su disposición. — I await your reply.

Le saluda atentamente — Yours sincerely / faithfully

Tenemos que pedir referencias.
We have to ask for references.

Una entrevista de trabajo

¿Por qué quiere ser … ?
Why do you want to be a … ?

Quiero ser … porque …
I want to be a … because …

Me gustaría trabajar de …
I would like to work as a …

¿Cuál es su experiencia laboral?
What work experience do you have?

Tengo experiencia en … — I have experience in ..

He trabajado como … — I have worked as a …
 director / gerente — manager
 representante de ventas — sales rep

He trabajado en marketing / mercadotecnia.
I have worked in marketing.

¿Qué cualidades personales tiene?
What are your personal qualities?

Soy creativo/a / ambicioso/a / trabajador/a.
I am creative / ambitious / hardworking.

¿Cuál es el horario de trabajo?
What are the hours of work?

De … a … / Desde … hasta … — From … until …

Worked example

LISTENING TRACK 51

Listen to the recording and answer the question **in English**.

What job interests Rosa? **(1 mark)**

flight attendant

Listen to the recording

– Quiero ser azafata porque me encanta trabajar con la gente. Tengo una entrevista con Iberia.

What does Rosa want to be? That is what the question is asking. If you have forgotten that **azafata** is 'flight attendant', use your cultural knowledge to help you: Rosa says she has an interview with the airline Iberia.

Learning vocabulary

The more vocabulary you know, the easier you will find listening activities. When learning vocabulary, don't waste valuable time going over words you already know or can guess.

Use different techniques to help you learn more difficult vocabulary:

- ✓ Write out the word and then copy it out several times.
- ✓ Ask someone to test you.
- ✓ Say the word aloud many times and record yourself saying it.
- ✓ Make associations – draw a picture or think of a story to help you remember the word.

Now try this

LISTENING TRACK 52

Listen to the recording

Listen to the whole recording from the worked example.
Which **three** statements are correct? Write the correct letters in the boxes. ☐ ☐ ☐ **(3 marks)**

A	Rosa never finds customers difficult.	D	Belén has worked with sick people in America.
B	Rosa is ambitious.	E	Belén has worked in a team.
C	Belén wants to be a vet.	F	Belén is not anti-social.

Careers and training

Be prepared to talk about professions that you are interested in.

Las profesiones y la formación

Tengo mucha ambición.
I have lots of ambition.
Quiero tener una licenciatura en …
I want to have a degree in …
Tengo la idea de hacer prácticas laborales.
I am thinking of doing an internship / work experience.
Estoy pensando en hacer un aprendizaje.
I am thinking about doing an apprenticeship.
Tengo que elegir la carrera adecuada.
I have to choose a suitable career.
(No) se necesita el bachillerato para ser …
You (don't) need A-levels to be …
Hay que realizar un curso de formación.
You have to do a training course.

Word families

Learning groups of words together and making mind maps is a great way of learning more vocabulary and preparing yourself for more difficult texts. When you learn a new noun, verb or adjective, see if there are any other related words.

> médico doctor ➡ medicina medicine

> estudiar to study ➡
> el estudiante student ➡
> los estudios studies

Worked example

SPEAKING

Prepare your answers to the following questions.
- ¿Qué hay en la foto?
- ¿Qué profesión te interesa más?
- ¿Qué piensas de trabajar como voluntario?
- ¿Cómo ha sido tu experiencia de trabajo?
- ¿Qué importancia tiene el pago de un trabajo, en tu opinión?

En la foto hay un médico que trabaja en un hospital. La profesión que más me gusta es la de profesora porque me gustan mucho los niños. Creo que trabajar como voluntario siempre vale la pena. Para mí es más importante ser feliz que ganar mucho dinero. El mes pasado trabajé como camarera y fue un trabajo bastante duro, pero ahora sé cómo hablar con los clientes.

AIMING HIGHER

En la foto se ve un médico que trabaja en un hospital. Ser médico no es una profesión que me interesa porque no quiero seguir estudiando ciencias. El año pasado trabajé como voluntario en una iglesia y aprendí muchas cosas que me ayudarán a lo largo de mi carrera. En verano trabajé de recepcionista en un camping y lo mejor fue que aprendí a atender a clientes descontentos. Me gustaría ser licenciada en arquitectura. Haría prácticas en una empresa internacional y aprendería a diseñar. La arquitectura es una profesión muy variada y también bien pagada, pero esto no es lo más importante para mí.

Exam alert

Think about the tenses to use for each bullet point and also how you can justify any opinions you give. The examiner may prompt you by asking ¿Por qué? or ¿Algo más?

It's important to justify your opinions: – **porque me gustan mucho los niños; para mí es más importante ser feliz**.

A good range of verbs in the conditional tense (**me gustaría**) and the impersonal **se** (**se ve un médico**) help to make this answer more complex. Using the irregular verb **hacer** in the conditional (**haría prácticas**) also shows good verb knowledge.

Now try this

SPEAKING
TRACK 53

Prepare answers to the following questions, then listen to the track and speak your answers in the pauses.
- ¿Qué profesión te gustaría hacer?
- En tu opinión, ¿qué importancia tiene el pago de un trabajo?

Listen to the recording

Nouns and articles

Here you'll find out about the gender of nouns and how to use the correct article.

Gender

Nouns are words that name things and people. Every Spanish noun has a gender – masculine (m) or feminine (f). If a word ends in -o or -a, it's easy to work out the gender.

ends in -o	masculine – el bolso
ends in -a	feminine – la pera

Exceptions:

el día	day	la foto	photo
el idioma	language	la moto	motorbike
el problema	problem	la mano	hand

For words ending in any other letter, you need to learn the word with the article. If you don't know the gender, look it up in a dictionary.

cine nm cinema

↗↖

noun masculine – so el cine

The definite article

The definite article ('the') changes to match the gender and number of the noun.

	Singular	Plural
Masculine	el libro	los libros
Feminine	la casa	las casas

The definite article is sometimes used in Spanish when we don't use it in English:

✓ with abstract nouns (things you can't see / touch)

El turismo es	Tourism is
importante.	important.

✓ with likes and dislikes

Me gusta el francés.   I like French.

✓ with days of the week to say 'on'

el domingo	on Sunday
los domingos	on Sundays

No me gustan nada las ciencias. I don't like science at all.

The indefinite article

The indefinite article ('a / an') changes to match the gender and number of the noun. In the plural, the English is 'some' or 'any'.

	Singular	Plural
Masculine	un libro	unos libros
Feminine	una casa	unas casas

The indefinite article is **not** used when you talk about jobs.

Soy profesor.   I'm a teacher.

Plurals

Plurals are easy to form in Spanish.

Singular	Plural
ends in a vowel un tomate	add -s unos tomates
ends in any consonant except -z la región	add -es las regiones
ends in -z el pez	drop z and add -ces los peces

Now try this

1 Make these nouns plural.
   (a) folleto ....
   (b) vez ....
   (c) tradición ....
   (d) café ....
   (e) actor ....

2 **El** or **la**? Use a dictionary to fill in the articles.
   (a) .... ciudad
   (b) .... pijama
   (c) .... pintor
   (d) .... educación
   (e) .... imagen

Adjectives

When using adjectives, you have to think about **agreement** and **position**.

Adjective agreement

Adjectives describe nouns. They must agree with the noun in gender (masculine or feminine) and number (singular or plural).

A dictionary shows the masculine form of an adjective. Make sure you don't forget to make it agree when it's feminine and / or plural!

las faldas amarillas   the yellow skirts

Adjective	Singular	Plural
ending in -o		
Masculine	alto	altos
Feminine	alta	altas
ending in -e		
Masculine	inteligente	inteligentes
Feminine	inteligente	inteligentes
ending in a consonant		
Masculine	azul	azules
Feminine	azul	azules

Note the exceptions:

ending in -or		
Masculine	hablador	habladores
Feminine	habladora	habladoras
adjectives of nationality ending in -s		
Masculine	inglés	ingleses
Feminine	inglesa	inglesas

Position of adjectives

Most Spanish adjectives come **after** the noun.

una falda azul   a blue skirt

These adjectives always come **before** the noun:

mucho	a lot	próximo	next
poco	a little	último	last
primero	first	alguno	some / any
segundo	second	ninguno	no
tercero	third		

Tengo muchos amigos. I have a lot of friends.

grande comes **before** the noun when it means 'great' rather than 'big'. It changes to **gran** before both masculine and feminine singular nouns.
Fue una gran película. It was a great film.

Short forms of adjectives

Some adjectives are shortened when they come before a masculine singular noun.

bueno	good	buen
malo	bad	mal
primero	first	primer
alguno	some / any	algún
ninguno	no	ningún

Pablo es un buen amigo. Pablo is a good friend.

Complete the text. (Look at the adjective endings to work out where they go.) Then translate the text into English.

bonitas   ruidosos   interesantes   ingleses   pequeña   habladora   históricos   simpática

Mallorca es una isla .... Tiene muchas playas .... En Mallorca hay muchos turistas .... La gente allí es muy .... y es muy .... Mallorca tiene muchos museos .... y muchos bares .... Se puede hacer muchas cosas ....

Possessives and pronouns

Use possessives to talk about who things belong to. Using pronouns will also help you sound more fluent.

Possessive adjectives

Possessive adjectives agree with the noun they describe, **not** the owner, e.g. sus botas – his boots.

	Singular	Plural
my	mi	mis
your	tu	tus
his / her / its	su	sus
our	nuestro / a	nuestros / as
your	vuestro / a	vuestros / as
their	su	sus

mis amigos
my friends

su colegio
their school

Possessive pronouns

These agree with the noun they replace, e.g. Su chaqueta es más elegante que la mía. His jacket is smarter than mine.

	Singular	
mine	el mío	la mía
yours	el tuyo	la tuya
his / hers / its	el suyo	la suya
ours	el nuestro	la nuestra
yours	el vuestro	la vuestra
theirs	el suyo	la suya
	Plural	
mine	los míos	las mías
yours	los tuyos	las tuyas
his / hers / its	los suyos	las suyas
ours	los nuestros	las nuestras
yours	los vuestros	las vuestras
theirs	los suyos	las suyas

Prepositional pronouns

These are used after prepositions.

para – for por – for sin – without a – to	mí – me	nosotros / as – us
	ti – you	vosotros / as – you
	él – him	ellos – them (m)
	ella – her	ellas – them (f)

Esta chaqueta es para ti.
This jacket is for you.

Note the accent on mí.

con + mí ➡ conmigo   with me
con + ti ➡ contigo   with you

The relative pronoun que

que ('which', 'that' or 'who') allows you to refer back to someone or something already mentioned. You must include it in Spanish, even when you might omit it in English.

El profesor que enseña francés.
The teacher who teaches French.
El libro que lee es español.
The book (that / which) he is reading is Spanish.

Now try this

Circle the correct form each time. Then translate the text into English.
Mis / Mi padrastro se llama Miguel. **Su / Sus** hijas son mis hermanastras. **Mi / Mis** hermanastra, **que / por** se llama Isabel, tiene un novio, Pablo. **Su / Sus** novio es menos guapo que **el mío / la mía**. Salgo con **él / ella** desde hace seis años. Isabel sale con **el suyo / las suyas** desde hace un mes.

Comparisons

If you're aiming for a higher grade, use structures like the comparative and superlative.

The comparative

The comparative is used to compare two things. It is formed as follows:

> más + adjective + que = more ... than
> menos + adjective + que = less ... than
> tan + adjective + como = as ... as

The adjective agrees with the noun it describes.

Madrid es más interesante que Leeds.
Madrid is more interesting than Leeds.
Pablo es menos alto que su hermano.
Pablo is shorter (less tall) than his brother.
Mi habitación es tan pequeña como la tuya.
My bedroom is as small as yours.

The superlative

The superlative is used to compare more than two things. It is formed as follows:

> el / la / los / las (+ noun) + más + adjective = the most ...
> el / la / los / las (+ noun) + menos + adjective = the least ...

The definite article and the adjective agree with the noun described.

El español es el idioma más interesante.
Spanish is the most interesting language.
Esta casa es la menos cara del pueblo.
This house is the least expensive in the village.

Irregulars

Learn these useful irregular forms:

Adjective	Comparative	Superlative
good	better	the best
bueno	mejor	el / la mejor los / las mejores
bad	worse	the worst
malo	peor	el / la peor los / las peores

Este hotel es el mejor de la región.
This hotel is the best in the region.
Los restaurantes de aquí son los peores.
The restaurants here are the worst.

Using -ísimo for emphasis

You can add -ísimo to the end of an adjective to make it stronger.

La chaqueta es carísima.
The jacket is very expensive.
El libro es malísimo.   The book is very bad.

La comida es riquísima.
The food is really delicious.

Don't forget to make adjectives agree!

Now try this

Complete the sentences with the correct comparative or superlative.

1 Este libro es .... de la trilogía. (*worst*)
2 Mis hermanos son .... amigos que tengo. (*best*)
3 La falda es .... de la tienda. (*prettiest*)
4 Este partido de fútbol es .... (*really boring*)
5 Carmen es .... jugadora. (*best*)
6 Este piso es .... que he visto hoy. (*ugliest*)
7 Pablo es .... que Juan. (*better looking*)
8 Mi hermana es .... que mi hermano. (*lazier*)

Other adjectives

Here you can revise demonstrative adjectives and some useful indefinite adjectives.

Demonstrative adjectives

Demonstrative adjectives ('this', 'that', 'these', 'those') agree with their noun in number and gender.

	Masculine	Feminine	
Singular	este	esta	this
Plural	estos	estas	these
Singular	ese	esa	that
Plural	esos	esas	those

este móvil	this mobile
esa calculadora	that calculator
esos chicos	those boys
estas chicas	these girls

Using different words for 'that' and 'those'

In Spanish there are two words for 'that' / 'those': ese and aquel. You use aquel to refer to something further away.

esa chica y aquel chico
that girl and that boy
(over there)

	Masculine	Feminine	
Singular	aquel	aquella	that
Plural	aquellos	aquellas	those

Indefinite adjectives

Indefinite adjectives come up in a lot of contexts, so make sure you know how to use them.

cada	each
otro	another
todo	all
mismo	same
algún / alguna	some / any

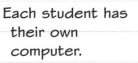

As with all other adjectives, remember to make them agree.
Exception: **cada** – it doesn't change.

Quisiera otra cerveza.	I would like another beer.
Todos los pasajeros estaban enfadados.	All the passengers were angry.
Llevamos la misma camiseta.	We're wearing the same T-shirt.
¿Tienes algún cuaderno?	Do you have any exercise book?
Cada estudiante tiene su ordenador.	Each student has their own computer.

Now try this

Translate into Spanish.
1 That boy is stupid.
2 This apple is tasty.
3 I want to buy those jeans.
4 That house over there is really big.
5 This film is boring.
6 I don't want that jumper – I want that cardigan over there.

Pronouns

Use pronouns to avoid repeating nouns – it helps make your Spanish more fluent and interesting.

Subject, direct object and indirect object

- The **subject** is the person / thing doing the action (shown by the verb).
- The **object** is the person / thing having the action (shown by the verb) done to them / it. It can be **direct** or **indirect**.

Subject	Verb	Direct object	Indirect object
Marisa	sends	the email	to David.
She	sends	it	to him.

Subject pronoun		Direct object pronoun		Indirect object pronoun	
I	yo	me	me	(to / for) me	me
you	tú	you	te	(to / for) you	te
he / it	él	him / it	lo	(to / for) him / it	le
she / it	ella	her / it	la	(to / for) her / it	le
we	nosotros / as	us	nos	(to / for) us	nos
you	vosotros / as	you	os	(to / for) you	os
they	ellos / ellas	them	los / las	(to / for) them	les

Subject pronouns aren't often used in Spanish because the verb ending is enough to show who is doing the action. They're sometimes used for **emphasis**.

A mí me gusta España, pero él quiere ir a Italia.   I like Spain but he wants to go to Italy.

Position of object pronouns

In general, object pronouns come:
- **before** the verb
- **after** a negative

La compré en el supermercado.	I bought it in the supermarket.
No la tengo.	I don't have it.
Nadie les escribe.	No one writes to them.

The object pronoun can be added to the infinitive in the near future tense.

Voy a comprarlo por Internet.   or
Lo voy a comprar por Internet.
I'm going to buy it online.

Object pronouns are attached to the end of a positive imperative.

¡Hazlo!   Do it!

Rewrite the sentences, replacing the words in bold with pronouns.
1 Voy a dar **el regalo** a mi padre.
2 Nunca escribo **a mi hermana**.
3 Voy a comprar **un libro**.
4 Pon **los tomates** en la bolsa.
5 Quiero decir **a Pablo** un secreto.

The present tense

This page covers all three types of regular verb and radical-changing verbs in the present tense.

Present tense (regular)

To form the present tense of regular verbs, replace the infinitive ending as follows:

	hablar – to speak	comer – to eat	vivir – to live
I	hablo	como	vivo
you	hablas	comes	vives
he / she / it	habla	come	vive
we	hablamos	comemos	vivimos
you	habláis	coméis	vivís
they	hablan	comen	viven

How to use the present tense

Use the present tense to talk about:
• what you are doing **now**
• what you do **regularly**
• what things are **like**.

You can also use the present tense to talk about planned future events.

Mañana voy a España. Tomorrow I'm going to Spain.

Remember that **usted** (polite / formal form of 'you') takes the endings for 'he / she / it'.
¿Habla inglés? Do you speak English?

Radical-changing verbs

In radical-changing verbs, the vowel in the syllable before the infinitive ending changes in the singular and 3rd person plural. There are three common groups.

	o → ue poder to be able	e → ie querer to want	e → i pedir to ask
I	puedo	quiero	pido
you	puedes	quieres	pides
he / she / it	puede	quiere	pide
we	podemos	queremos	pedimos
you	podéis	queréis	pedís
they	pueden	quieren	piden

Other examples of radical-changing verbs:

u / o → ue	e → ie
jugar → juego to play	empezar → empiezo to start
dormir → duermo to sleep	entender → entiendo to understand
volver → vuelvo to return	pensar → pienso to think
encontrar → encuentro to find	preferir → prefiero to prefer

¿Quieres salir esta noche?
Do you want to go out tonight?
Rafa juega al tenis todos los días.
Rafa plays tennis every day.

Now try this

Complete the sentences using the present tense. Then translate the sentences into English.

1 No .... música clásica. *escuchar (I)*
2 Mis padres .... inglés. *hablar*
3 Mi amigo .... al baloncesto conmigo. *jugar*
4 ¿.............. ir al cine conmigo esta noche? *querer (you singular informal)*
5 Siempre .... fruta para estar sanos. *comer (we)*
6 Siempre .... dinero en la calle. *encontrar (they)*
7 ¿.............. en el campo? *vivir (you plural informal)*
8 Mi hermano .... en su propio dormitorio. *dormir*

Reflexive verbs (present)

Reflexive verbs include a reflexive pronoun which refers back to the person doing the action.

Present tense (regular)

Reflexive verbs have the same endings as other present tense verbs but contain a reflexive pronoun. Some are also radical-changing verbs.

	lavarse to wash	vestirse to get dressed
I	me lavo	me visto
you	te lavas	te vistes
he / she / it / you (sing. polite)	se lava	se viste
we	nos lavamos	nos vestimos
you	os laváis	os vestís
they / you (pl. polite)	se lavan	se visten

In the infinitive form, the pronoun can be added to the end of the verb.
Voy a levantarme.   I'm going to get up.

> You can use the reflexive pronoun se to create an impersonal construction:
> Aquí no se puede nadar.
> You cannot swim here.
> Se necesita gente con experiencia.
> People with experience are needed.

Useful reflexive verbs

Reflexive verbs are particularly useful when you describe your daily routines. They are also useful for describing some emotions.

acordarse de	me acuerdo de	I remember
arrepentirse de	me arrepiento de	I regret
bañarse	me baño	I take a bath
divertirse	me divierto	I enjoy myself
ducharse	me ducho	I take a shower
enfadarse	me enfado	I get angry
levantarse	me levanto	I get up
llamarse	me llamo	I am called
maquillarse	me maquillo	I put on make-up
parecerse a	me parezco a	I look like
preocuparse	me preocupo	I worry
sentarse	me siento	I sit down
quejarse	me quejo	I complain

Nos vestimos.
We get dressed.

Mi hermana se cepilla los dientes.
My sister brushes her teeth.

Mis amigas se maquillan en casa.
My friends put on their make-up at home.

¿A qué hora te duchas?
What time do you take a shower?

Now try this

Complete the sentences with the correct reflexive pronouns.

1 .... despierto temprano.
2 Mi hermano.............. afeita a las siete.
3 Mañana voy a peinar.............. antes de desayunar.
4 .... acostamos siempre a la misma hora.
5 ¿A qué hora.............. levantas normalmente?
6 Mis padres.............. duchan después de desayunar.

Irregular verbs (present)

Make sure you know how to use these irregular verbs correctly.

The verbs ir and tener

These key verbs are irregular in the present tense.

	ir – to go
I	voy
you	vas
he / she / it / you (sing. polite)	va
we	vamos
you	vais
they / you (pl. polite)	van

	tener – to have
I	tengo
you	tienes
he / she / it / you (sing. polite)	tiene
we	tenemos
you	tenéis
they / you (pl. polite)	tienen

Tengo que hacer los deberes y luego voy al cine.
I have to do my homework and then I'm going to the cinema.

Other irregular verbs

Some other useful verbs are also irregular in the present tense.

decir – to say	digo, dices, dice, decimos, decís, dicen
oír – to hear	oigo, oyes, oye, oímos, oís, oyen
venir – to come	vengo, vienes, viene, venimos, venís, vienen

Some verbs are irregular to keep the pronunciation correct.
proteger – **to protect** ➡ protejo – I protect
coger – **to take** ➡ cojo – I take

Irregular 'I' forms

Some verbs are irregular in the 'I' form only.

conducir	to drive	➡	conduzco
conocer	to know / meet	➡	conozco
dar	to give	➡	doy
hacer	to make / do	➡	hago
poner	to put	➡	pongo
saber	to know	➡	sé
salir	to go out	➡	salgo
traer	to bring	➡	traigo

Now try this

Complete these sentences with the correct form of the verb in brackets. Then translate them into English.

1 Yo .... a las siete y media para ir al concierto. (*salir*)

2 Mis primos .... los ojos azules y son rubios. (*tener*)

3 Me gusta mucho ir a la playa pero no .... nadar. (*saber*)

4 Siempre .... el autobús cuando voy al instituto. (*coger*)

5 Mis amigos .... los deberes en la biblioteca pero yo los .... en casa. (*hacer*)

6 Creo que .... muy bien, ¡pero mi padre cree que no! (*conducir*)

Ser and estar

Spanish has two verbs meaning 'to be': ser and estar. Both are irregular – you need to know them well.

The present tense of ser

	ser – to be
I am	soy
you are	eres
he / she / it is	es
we are	somos
you are	sois
they are	son

> Roberto es un chico feliz.
> Roberto is a happy boy.

When to use ser

Use ser for **permanent** things.

- nationality

Soy inglés.	I'm English.

- occupation

Es profesor.	He's a teacher.

- colour and size

Es rojo. Es pequeño.	It's red. It's small.

- personality

Son habladoras.	They're talkative.

- telling the time

Son las tres.	It's three o'clock.

The present tense of estar

	estar – to be
I am	estoy
you are	estás
he / she / it is	está
we are	estamos
you are	estáis
they are	están

> Hoy Alicia está aburridísima.
> Alicia is really bored today.

When to use estar

Use estar for **temporary** things and **locations**.

- illness

Estoy enfermo.	I'm unwell.

- appearance (temporary)

Estás guapo.	You look handsome.

- feelings (temporary)

Estoy contento porque gané la lotería.
I'm happy because I won the lottery.

- location

Madrid está en España.	Madrid is in Spain.

> Watch out for this one!
> ser listo   to be clever
> estar listo   to be ready

Now try this

Complete the sentences with **ser** or **estar** in the present tense.

1 ¿Dónde .... la parada de autobús?
2 Valencia .... grande e interesante.
3 Mi hermano .... abogado.
4 .... constipado. *(I)*
5 Las botas .... negras.
6 Mi mejor amiga .... escocesa.
7 Hoy mis amigos no .... contentos porque tienen una prueba.
8 María .... guapa esta noche con su vestido nuevo.

The gerund

Gerunds are '-ing' words. Use this page to review how they're formed and used.

The gerund

To form the gerund of regular verbs, replace the infinitive ending as follows:

hablar – hablando
comer – comiendo
vivir – viviendo

Common irregular gerunds:

caer	cayendo	falling
dormir	durmiendo	sleeping
leer	leyendo	reading
oír	oyendo	hearing
pedir	pidiendo	asking (for something)
poder	pudiendo	being able to
reír	riendo	laughing

Está jugando al fútbol.
He's playing football.

Uses of the gerund

You use the gerund:

- to give more information about how something was or is being done
  Voy andando al instituto.
  I go to school on foot.

- after ir (to go), seguir (to keep on) and continuar (to continue)
  Sigo aprendiendo informática porque es útil.
  I keep studying ICT because it's useful.

- to form the present continuous and imperfect continuous tenses (see below).

You can't always translate an '-ing' verb in English by the gerund in Spanish, e.g.
Aprender español es emocionante.
Learning Spanish is exciting.
Vamos a salir mañana.
We're leaving tomorrow.

Present continuous tense

The present continuous describes what is happening at this moment:
present tense of estar + the gerund

	estar – to be	gerund
I	estoy	
you	estás	haciendo saliendo durmiendo riendo
he / she / it	está	
we	estamos	
you	estáis	
they	están	

Estoy viendo la televisión. I'm watching TV.

Imperfect continous tense

This tense describes what was happening at a certain moment in the past:
imperfect tense of estar + the gerund

	estar – to be	gerund
I	estaba	
you	estabas	visitando estudiando escribiendo buscando
he / she / it	estaba	
we	estábamos	
you	estabais	
they	estaban	

Estaba leyendo.   I was reading.

Now try this

Rewrite the sentences using the present continuous tense. Write them again using the imperfect continuous.

1　Juego al tenis.
2　Escribo un correo electrónico.
3　Habla con mi amigo Juan.
4　Duerme en la cama.
5　Como cereales.
6　Tomo el sol en la playa.
7　Navegan por Internet.
8　¿Cantas en tu habitación?

The preterite tense

The preterite tense is used to talk about completed actions in the past.

Preterite tense (regular)

To form the preterite tense of regular verbs, replace the infinitive ending as follows:

	hablar – to speak	comer – to eat	vivir – to live
I	hablé	comí	viví
you	hablaste	comiste	viviste
he / she / it	habló	comió	vivió
we	hablamos	comimos	vivimos
you	hablasteis	comisteis	vivisteis
they	hablaron	comieron	vivieron

Be careful – accents can be significant.
Hablo. I speak.
Habló. He / She spoke.

Preterite tense (irregular)

	ir – to go ser – to be	hacer – to do	ver – to see
I	fui	hice	vi
you	fuiste	hiciste	viste
he / she / it	fue	hizo	vio
we	fuimos	hicimos	vimos
you	fuisteis	hicisteis	visteis
they	fueron	hicieron	vieron

The verbs **ir** and **ser** have the same forms in the preterite. Use the context to work out which is meant.

How to use the preterite tense

You use the preterite to describe completed actions in the past.

El año pasado viajé a los Estados Unidos.
Last year I travelled to the United States.

Recognise and use a range of preterite tense time expressions.

ayer	yesterday
anoche	last night
anteayer / antes de ayer	the day before yesterday
el verano pasado	last summer
la semana pasada	last week

Useful irregular preterite forms to know:

andar	anduve	I walked
dar	di	I gave
decir	dije	I said
estar	estuve	I was
poner	puse	I put
saber	supe	I knew
tener	tuve	I had
venir	vine	I came

Note these verbs with irregular spelling in 'I' form only:

cruzar	crucé	I crossed
empezar	empecé	I started
jugar	jugué	I played
llegar	llegué	I arrived
tocar	toqué	I played

Now try this

Identify the tense in each sentence (present or preterite). Then translate the sentences into English.

1 Voy a Italia.
2 Llegué a las seis.
3 Navego por Internet.
4 Escuchó música.
5 Fue a una fiesta que fue guay.
6 Hizo frío y llovió un poco.
7 Vimos a Pablo en el mercado.
8 Jugué al baloncesto en la playa.

The imperfect tense

The imperfect is another verb tense used to talk about the past.

Imperfect tense (regular)

To form the imperfect tense of regular verbs, replace the infinitive ending as follows:

	hablar – to speak	comer – to eat	vivir – to live
I	hablaba	comía	vivía
you	hablabas	comías	vivías
he / she / it	hablaba	comía	vivía
we	hablábamos	comíamos	vivíamos
you	hablabais	comíais	vivíais
they	hablaban	comían	vivían

-er and -ir verbs have the same endings.

Try to use both the **imperfect** and the **preterite** in your work to aim for a higher grade.

How to use the imperfect tense

You use the imperfect to talk about:
- what people used to do / how things used to be

Antes no separaba la basura.
I didn't use to sort the rubbish before.

- repeated actions in the past

Jugaba al tenis todos los días.
I played tennis every day.

- descriptions in the past

El hotel era caro.
The hotel was expensive.

Hacía de canguro. Ahora trabajo como jardinera.
I used to babysit. Now I work as a gardener.

Imperfect tense (irregular)

Only three verbs are irregular:

	ir – to go	ser – to be	ver – to see
I	iba	era	veía
you	ibas	eras	veías
he / she / it	iba	era	veía
we	íbamos	éramos	veíamos
you	ibais	erais	veíais
they	iban	eran	veían

Preterite or imperfect?

- Use the preterite tense for a **single / completed** event in the past.
  Ayer visité Brighton.
  Yesterday I visited Brighton.
- Use the imperfect tense for **repeated / continuous** events in the past.
  En Brighton había un castillo.
  There used to be a castle in Brighton.

Now try this

Complete the sentences with the imperfect or preterite tense, as appropriate.

1 Mi madre .... para Iberia todos los veranos. *trabajar*

2 Ayer .... mucho chocolate. *comer (I)*

3 Antes .... a Grecia a menudo con mis padres. *ir (I)*

4 En los años setenta .... más paro que ahora. *haber*

5 El verano pasado .... Marruecos por primera vez. *visitar (I)*

6 De pequeño mi hermanito .... siempre. *llorar*

The future tense

To aim for a higher grade, you need to use a future tense as well as the present and past.

Future tense

To form the future tense of most verbs, add the following endings to the infinitive:

ir – to go			
I	iré	we	iremos
you	irás	you	iréis
he / she / it	irá	they	irán

Some verbs use a different stem. You need to memorise these:

decir to say ➡ diré I will say
haber there is / are ➡ habrá there will be
hacer to make / do ➡ haré I will make / do
poder to be able to ➡ podré I will be able to
querer to want ➡ querré I will want
saber to know ➡ sabré I will know
salir to leave ➡ saldré I will leave
tener to have ➡ tendré I will have
venir to come ➡ vendré I will come

Immediate future tense

You form the immediate future tense as follows:

present tense of ir + a + infinitive

	ir – to go		infinitive
I	voy		
you	vas		mandar
he / she / it	va	a	bailar
we	vamos		salir
you	vais		venir
they	van		

¿Vas a comer algo?
Are you going to have something to eat?

Vamos a ir a la fiesta.
We're going to go to the festival / party.

Recognise and use a range of time expressions that indicate the future,
e.g. mañana   tomorrow,   mañana por la mañana   tomorrow morning,
el mes que viene   next month,   el próximo viernes   next Friday.

Using the future tense

Use the future tense to talk about what will happen in the future.

El año que viene será difícil encontrar un buen trabajo.
Next year it will be difficult to find a good job.
Si trabajo como voluntario, mejoraré el mundo.
If I work as a volunteer, I will make the world better.

Using the immediate future tense

You use the immediate future tense to say what is going to happen. It is used to talk about future plans.

En Barcelona va a comprar recuerdos.
He's going to buy souvenirs in Barcelona.
Voy a salir esta tarde.
I'm going to go out this afternoon.

Now try this

1 Rewrite the sentences using the future tense.
   (a) Nunca fumo.
   (b) Ayudo a los demás.
   (c) Cambiamos el mundo.
   (d) Trabajo en un aeropuerto.

2 Rewrite the sentences using the immediate future tense.
   (a) Salgo a las seis.
   (b) Soy médico.
   (c) Va a España.
   (d) Mañana juego al tenis.

The conditional tense

The conditional is used to describe what you **would do** or what **would happen** in the future.

The conditional

To form the conditional, you add the following endings to the infinitive:

	hablar – to speak
I	hablaría
you	hablarías
he / she / it	hablaría
we	hablaríamos
you	hablaríais
they	hablarían

The endings are the same for **all** verbs.

Some verbs use a different stem.

decir to say	➡	diría
haber there is / are	➡	habría
hacer to do	➡	haría
poder to be able to	➡	podría
querer to want	➡	querría
saber to know	➡	sabría
salir to leave	➡	saldría
tener to have	➡	tendría
venir to come	➡	vendría

Un sistema de alquiler de bicicletas sería una idea muy buena.
A bike hire scheme would be a really good idea.

Use **poder** in the conditional + the infinitive to say what you **could** do.
Podríamos ir a Ibiza.   We could go to Ibiza.

Use **deber** in the conditional + the infinitive to say what you **should** do.
Debería fumar menos cigarrillos.
I should smoke fewer cigarettes.

Expressing future intent

The conditional can be used to express future intent.
Use gustar in the conditional + the infinitive.
En el futuro ...

me gustaría ir a Australia.
I'd like to go to Australia.

me gustaría ser bailarina.
I'd like to be a dancer.

me gustaría comprarme un coche nuevo.
I'd like to buy a new car.

You can also use me encantaría, e.g.
Me encantaría ser futbolista.
I'd love to be a footballer.

Now try this

Rewrite the text, changing the verbs in bold to the conditional.
Para mantenerme en forma **bebo** mucha agua. **Hago** mucho ejercicio y **practico** mucho deporte. Nunca **tomo** drogas y no **bebo** alcohol. **Como** mucha fruta y **me acuesto** temprano – siempre **duermo** ocho horas, gracias a eso **llevo** una vida sana.

Perfect and pluperfect

The perfect and pluperfect are two more tenses used to talk about the past. You should be able to use both.

Perfect tense

To form the perfect tense, use the present tense of haber + past participle:

	haber – to have
I	he
you	has
he / she / it	ha
we	hemos
you	habéis
they	han

Pluperfect tense

To form the pluperfect tense, use the imperfect tense of haber + past participle:

	haber – to have
I	había
you	habías
he / she / it	había
we	habíamos
you	habíais
they	habían

Past participle

To form the past participle, replace the infinitive ending as follows:

hablar ➡ hablado
comer ➡ comido
vivir ➡ vivido

Ha comprado un nuevo CD.   He has bought a new CD.
No habían salido.   They hadn't gone out.
Había hecho mis deberes.   I had done my homework.
¿Has visto a María?   Have you seen María?

Here are some common irregular past participles:

abrir	➡ abierto	opened
decir	➡ dicho	said
escribir	➡ escrito	written
hacer	➡ hecho	done
poner	➡ puesto	put
romper	➡ roto	broken
ver	➡ visto	seen
volver	➡ vuelto	returned

Using the perfect tense

The perfect tense describes what someone **has done** or something that **has happened**.
He ido a la piscina.
I have been to the swimming pool.

Using the pluperfect tense

The pluperfect tense describes what someone **had done** or something that **had happened** at a particular time in the past.
Cuando llegó, la orquesta había empezado ya.
When he arrived, the orchestra had already started.

Now try this

Rewrite the sentences in the correct order. Identify the tense in each one: perfect or pluperfect?

1 visitado / he / . / novio / mi / con / Palma
2 ayuda / hecho / deberes / mi / . / han / sus / con
3 ido / . / habíamos / Pablo / con / supermercado / al
4 amor / de / carta / una / . / escrito / ha / hermana / mi
5 has / ¿ / abrigo / mi / visto / ?
6 llegó / cuando / , / primos / ya / comido / . / mis / habían /

Giving instructions

You use the imperative to give instructions and commands.

The imperative

The imperative changes its form depending on two things:
• whether the command is positive or negative
• who receives the command.

Toma la primera calle a la izquierda.   Take the first street on the left.
Poned la mesa.   Lay the table.
No tiréis basura al suelo.   Don't throw litter on the floor.

> Commands may be given to one person (singular) or more than one person (plural). They may also be informal or formal.

Positive commands

The tú command (informal singular) is formed by removing the -s from the tú form of the present tense.

Infinitive	Tú present tense	Tú imperative
hablar	hablas	habla
comer	comes	come
vivir	vives	vive

The vosotros command (informal plural) is formed by taking the infinitive, removing the -r and adding -d.

Infinitive	Vosotros imperative
hablar	hablad
comer	comed
vivir	vivid

To give a **formal** command (usted or ustedes forms), you **always** use the present subjunctive. For information on how to form the present subjunctive, go to page 99.

¡No hable!   Don't speak! (usted form)
¡Coman!   Eat! (ustedes form)

Irregular imperatives

These verbs have irregular tú forms in the imperative.

decir ➡ ¡Di!   Say!
hacer ➡ ¡Haz! Do!
ir   ➡ ¡Ve!   Go!
dar   ➡ ¡Da!   Give!
salir ➡ ¡Sal! Leave!
tener ➡ ¡Ten! Have!

Negative commands

You use the present subjunctive to form **all** negative commands. For more information on the present subjunctive, go to page 99.

¡No grites!   Don't shout! (tú form)
¡No habléis!   Don't talk! (vosotros form)
¡No fume!   Don't smoke! (usted form)
¡No beban!   Don't drink! (ustedes form)

¡No saques fotos!
Don't take photos!

Now try this

Translate the instructions into English.
1 Escríbeme.
2 Espera a tu hermana.
3 No me digas nada.
4 ¡No gritéis!
5 Haz clic aquí.
6 ¡No saques fotos!
7 Contestad a las preguntas.
8 No lo dejes todo para el último momento.

No destruyan la selva.
Don't destroy the rainforest.

The present subjunctive

The subjunctive form of the verb is used in certain constructions.

The present subjunctive

To form the present subjunctive, replace the -o ending of the 'I' form of the present tense as follows:

	hablar – to speak	comer – to eat	vivir – to live
I	hable	coma	viva
you	hables	comas	vivas
he / she / it	hable	coma	viva
we	hablemos	comamos	vivamos
you	habléis	comáis	viváis
they	hablen	coman	vivan

-er and -ir verbs have the same endings.

This rule works for most verbs which are irregular in the present tense.

Infinitive	Present	Subjunctive
hacer	hago	haga
tener	tengo	tenga

Two verbs, ir and ser, are different.

	ir – to go	ser – to be
I	vaya	sea
you	vayas	seas
he / she / it	vaya	sea
we	vayamos	seamos
you	vayáis	seáis
they	vayan	sean

How to use the subjunctive

The subjunctive is used:

* to express doubt or uncertainty

No creo que tenga tiempo.
I don't think I have time.

* to deny that information is true

No es verdad que sea adicto al ordenador.
It isn't true that I'm a computer addict.

* after ojalá

¡Ojalá (que) nadie me vea!
Let's hope no one sees me!

* after cuando when talking about the future

Cuando sea mayor, quiero hacer caída libre.
When I'm older, I want to do skydiving.

* to express a wish with querer que

¿Quieres que nos vayamos?
Do you want us to go?

Remember: the subjunctive is also used in some imperatives – see page 98.

Remember: the subjunctive is also used in some imperatives – see page 98.

Now try this

Translate the sentences into English.
1 Cuando vaya a la universidad, estudiaré francés.
2 No creo que tu amigo sea guapo.
3 Cuando tenga dieciocho años, me tomaré un año sabático.
4 Quiero que hables con Pablo.
5 No es verdad que la comida inglesa sea horrible.
6 No creo que Italia sea el mejor equipo de fútbol.

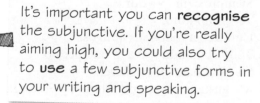

It's important you can **recognise** the subjunctive. If you're really aiming high, you could also try to **use** a few subjunctive forms in your writing and speaking.

Negatives

You need to be able to understand and use negatives in all parts of the exam.

Negatives

no	not
no ... nada	nothing / not anything
no ... nunca	never
no ... jamás	never
no ... ni ... ni ...	not ... (either) ... or ...
no ... tampoco	not ... either
no ... ningún / ninguna	no / not any
no ... nadie	no one / nobody

How to use negatives

- The simplest way to make a sentence negative in Spanish is to use no. It comes before the verb.
  No nadé en el mar.
  I didn't swim in the sea.

- Negative expressions with two parts sandwich the verb (i.e. they go round it).
  Dicen que no nieva nunca en Málaga.
  They say that it never snows in Malaga.

- Two-part negative expressions can be shortened and put before the verb for emphasis.
  Nadie está aquí. No one's here.

No tengo nada que ponerme.
I don't have anything to wear.

No quiero ni nadar ni hacer yoga.
I don't want to swim or do yoga.

No me gustan los perros tampoco.
I don't like dogs either.

Expressions to use with negatives

Ya no estudio alemán.	I no longer study German.
No bebo agua sino zumo de naranja.	I don't drink water but orange juice.
Todavía no ha estudiado mucho.	He hasn't studied a lot yet.
Espero que no.	I hope not.
Creo que no.	I don't think so.
Claro que no.	Of course not.

Use a range of negatives in your Spanish to aim for a higher grade.

Now try this

Make the sentences negative, giving the opposite meanings. Then translate the original sentences into English.

1 Siempre como verduras.
2 Tengo un libro.
3 Conozco a todos sus amigos.
4 Todo el mundo juega al baloncesto.
5 Siempre hago mis deberes.
6 Me gusta navegar por Internet y descargar música.
7 Tiene todo.
8 Tengo muchos amigos en Londres.

Special verbs

Verbs like gustar are used mainly in the 3rd person. You'll need them for a lot of topics, so they're worth learning carefully.

Present tense of gustar

Me gusta ('I like') literally translates as 'it pleases me'. The thing that does the pleasing (i.e. the thing I like) is the subject.

Me gusta este libro.   I like this book.

If the subject is plural, use me gustan.

Me gustan estos libros.

I like these books.

The pronoun changes as follows:

me	gusta(n)	I like
te	gusta(n)	you like
le	gusta(n)	he / she / it likes
nos	gusta(n)	we like
os	gusta(n)	you like
les	gusta(n)	they like

encantar behaves in the same way as gustar:
Le encanta la música rock. He loves rock music.

Preterite tense of gustar

In the preterite:

me gusta ➡ me gustó

me gustan ➡ me gustaron

The pronouns in the other forms are the same as for the present tense.

Nos gustó la comida española.
We liked Spanish food.
Le gustaron las tiendas.
He / She liked the shops.

To talk about other people's likes / dislikes, you need a before their name:
A Ignacio le gusta el deporte. Ignacio likes sport.

If you're aiming for higher grades, use **gustar** in the preterite to extend your language range.

Other verbs like gustar

Other verbs follow the same pattern as gustar: pronoun + 3rd person singular / plural of the verb

doler	me duele(n)	My ... hurt(s)
quedar	me queda(n)	I have ... left
hacer falta	me hace(n) falta	I need ...
faltar	me falta	I'm missing ...

Me duele el tobillo.
My ankle hurts.

Les quedan 20 euros.
They have 20 euros left.
¿Te hace falta una cuchara?
Do you need a spoon?
Le faltan dos libros.
He / She's missing two books.

Now try this

Complete the sentences.

1 .... el brazo. *(doler, I)*

2 .... el queso. *(gustar, she)*

3 .... los españoles. *(gustar, I, preterite)*

4 .... un cuchillo. *(hacer falta, they)*

5 .... los pies. *(doler, he)*

6 .... el español. *(encantar, I)*

7 .... cinco euros. *(quedar, we)*

8 .... las películas francesas. *(gustar, María)*

Por and para

Por and para are both often translated by 'for' in English. Learn the different contexts in which they're used.

Using por

You use por for:

- **cause**
  Pagué cien euros por el vuelo.
  I paid €100 for the flight.
  El vuelo fue cancelado por la huelga.
  The flight was cancelled because of the strike.

- action **on behalf of** someone
  Lo hizo por mí.   She did it for me.

- **rates**
  Gano seis euros por hora.
  I earn €6 per hour.

- means of **communication**
  Me llamó por teléfono.
  He called me on the phone.

- unspecified periods of **time**
  Me quedaré en Barcelona por poco tiempo.
  I will stay in Barcelona for a short time.

Using para

You use para for:

- **purpose** (it can often be translated by 'in order to')
  Llevamos una botella de agua fría para el viaje.
  We're taking a bottle of cold water for the journey.
  Voy a utilizar mi tarjeta de crédito para pagar el hotel.
  I'm going to use my credit card to pay for the hotel.
  Voy a comprar unos regalos para mi familia.
  I'm going to buy some presents for my family.

- **destination**
  Ha salido para Bilbao.
  She has left for Bilbao.

- specific **time** periods or **deadlines** in the future
  Quisiera una habitación para quince días.
  I would like a room for a fortnight.

Try writing out phrases with **por** and **para**, using one colour for **por** each time and another colour for **para**. Then when you're trying to remember which one to use, try to visualise the colour.

Now try this

1 Choose **por** or **para** to complete these sentences.

(a) Voy a ir a Madrid .... hacer compras.

(b) El tren .... Sevilla sale a las seis.

(c) Gracias .... el regalo.

(d) Los deberes son .... mañana.

(e) Este regalo es .... mi profesor.

(f) Voy a llamarle .... teléfono.

(g) Una azafata gana veinte euros .... hora.

2 Tick the sentences which are correct. Correct those that are wrong.

(a) Salimos por Nueva York.

(b) Solo estudio para la mañana.

(c) Por ganar dinero hay que trabajar duro.

(d) Voy a hacerlo para ti.

(e) Juego al fútbol para divertirme.

(f) Estas flores son por mi novia.

(g) Gano dinero para comprar un móvil nuevo.

(h) En el 18 por ciento de las casas hay una motocicleta.

Questions and exclamations

Being able to use questions and exclamations is essential in most topics.

How to ask questions

To ask yes / no questions, use the same language as you would to say the sentence and:
- if you're writing, add question marks
- if you're speaking, use a rising intonation at the end.

¿Estudias español? →

Do you study Spanish?

¿Quieres ir al polideportivo?

Do you want to go to the leisure centre?

> Remember the ¿ at the start.

To ask open questions, use a question word.

¿Cuándo?	When?
¿Dónde?	Where?
¿Adónde?	Where to?
¿De dónde?	From where?
¿Cuánto / a?	How much?
¿Cuántos / as?	How many?
¿Qué?	What?
¿Por qué?	Why?
¿Cómo?	How?
¿Cuál(es)?	Which (ones)?
¿Quién(es)?	Who?
¿Cuál (de estos libros) te gusta más?	Which (one of these books) do you like more?

> Don't forget the accents on question words.

Using exclamations

Using exclamations is a good way to extend how you give opinions in your spoken and written Spanish. Here are some useful examples:

¡Qué lástima!	What a shame!
¡Qué problema!	What a problem!
¡Qué raro!	How strange!
¡Qué va!	No way!
¡Qué rollo!	How boring!

> Remember the ¡ at the start as well as at the end.

¡Qué emocionante!
How exciting!

¡Qué difícil!
How difficult!

Question tag

English has a lot of different ways of asking for confirmation, e.g. 'doesn't he?', 'haven't they?', 'can't you?'. In Spanish it's much easier. You just put verdad at the end of a question.

¿Pablo es tu novio, verdad?

Pablo is your boyfriend, isn't he?

Now try this

Match the sentence halves.

1 ¿Cuál   **a** cuesta?
2 ¿Adónde   **b** personas hay en tu clase?
3 ¿Quién   **c** te llamas?
4 ¿Dónde   **d** es tu asignatura preferida?
5 ¿Cuánto   **e** está Jaén?
6 ¿Cuántas   **f** fuiste de vacaciones el año pasado?
7 ¿Cómo   **g** es tu cumpleaños?
8 ¿Cuándo   **h** es tu pintor preferido?

Connectives and adverbs

Use connectives to link phrases and sentences, and use adverbs to add detail to your Spanish.

Connectives

Connectives are words that link phrases and sentences together. You can use them to make your Spanish more varied and interesting.

Hago atletismo pero no me gusta mucho.
I do athletics but I don't like it much.

además	as well / besides / moreover
antes (de)	before
así que	so / therefore
después (de)	after
entonces	then
mientras	while
o	or
pero	but
por desgracia	unfortunately
por eso	therefore
por una parte	on the one hand
por otra parte	on the other hand
porque	because
pues	then / since
si	if
sin embargo	however
también	also
y / e	and

Another good way to improve your work is to extend your sentences using clauses with: que that / who, donde where, cuando when, como like / as, cuyo whose.

Adverbs

Adverbs describe how an action is done – they give you more detail about verbs. Many adverbs are formed by adding -mente to the feminine form of the adjective
lento ➡ lenta ➡ lentamente   slowly
Adverbs usually come **after** the verb.

Monta a caballo frecuentemente.
She goes riding frequently.

Sometimes they come **before** the verb, for emphasis.

Irregular adverbs

Here are some useful irregular adverbs to learn:

bastante	enough	despacio	slowly
bien	well	mal	badly
demasiado	too	mucho	a lot
	much	poco	a little
deprisa	fast	ya	already

Siempre nado los martes.
I always go swimming on Tuesdays.

Now try this

1 Connect the sentence pairs with an appropriate connective.
   (a) Nunca voy a París. Es aburrido.
   (b) Jugaba al baloncesto. Juan hacía patinaje.
   (c) Estudiaré. Iré a la universidad.
   (d) Nos gustaría ir a la playa. Está lloviendo.

2 Make adverbs from the adjectives. Translate them into English.
   (a) tranquilo
   (b) perfecto
   (c) difícil
   (d) severo

Numbers

Numbers come up in almost **every** context. Make sure you know them well.

Numbers

1	uno	11	once	21	veintiuno	100	cien
2	dos	12	doce	22	veintidós	101	ciento uno
3	tres	13	trece	30	treinta	200	doscientos / as
4	cuatro	14	catorce	31	treinta y uno	333	trescientos / as
5	cinco	15	quince	32	treinta y dos		treinta y tres
6	seis	16	dieciséis	40	cuarenta	1000	mil
7	siete	17	diecisiete	50	cincuenta		
8	ocho	18	dieciocho	60	sesenta		
9	nueve	19	diecinueve	70	setenta		
10	diez	20	veinte	80	ochenta		
				90	noventa		

Numbers ending in **uno** need to agree. They drop the -o before a masculine noun: veintiún años

The pattern for 31, 32, etc., is the same for 41, 42, etc.

The hundreds need to agree. Note: there are some irregular forms:
500 – **quinientos**,
700 – **setecientos**,
900 – **novecientos**.

Ordinal numbers

When used with nouns, ordinal numbers agree.

primero	first	sexto	sixth
segundo	second	séptimo	seventh
tercero	third	octavo	eighth
cuarto	fourth	noveno	ninth
quinto	fifth	décimo	tenth

Primero and tercero change to primer and tercer before a masculine singular noun, e.g. el tercer día.

Ordinals are **not** used for dates except for the 1st.

You don't use a capital letter for the months.

Telling the time

Son las cinco.	It's five o'clock.
A las diez.	At ten o'clock.

One o'clock is different:
Es la una.

3.05 las tres y cinco
3.15 las tres y cuarto
3.30 las tres y media
3.45 las cuatro menos cuarto
3.55 las cuatro menos cinco

Dates

Dates follow this pattern:
13 December 1978 =
el trece de diciembre de mil novecientos setenta y ocho
21 July 2016
el veintiuno de julio de dos mil dieciséis
The first of the month can be either:
el primero de abril or el uno de abril.

Now try this

Write the numbers, dates and times in Spanish.
1 8.40 **2** 465 **3** 12 June 2014 **4** 7th **5** 11.30 **6** 76 **7** 1 January 1997 **8** 3rd

Vocabulary

This section starts with general terms that are useful in a wide variety of situations and then divides vocabulary into groups under the three main topics covered in this revision guide:

1 High-frequency language   **2** Identity and culture   **3** Local, national, international and global areas of interest   **4** Current and future study and employment

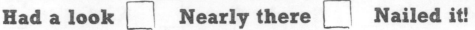 Sections to be learned by all candidates   ◐ Sections to be learned by Higher candidates only

Learning vocabulary is essential preparation for your reading and listening exams. Don't try to learn too much at once – concentrate on learning and testing yourself on a page at a time.

1 High-frequency language

Verbs A–C

abrir	to open
acabar	to finish
aceptar	to accept
acompañar	to accompany
aconsejar	to advise
agradecer	to thank
ahorrar	to save
almorzar	to have lunch
alquilar	to rent, hire
amar	to love
andar	to walk
añadir	to add
aprender	to learn
aprovecharse de	to take advantage of
arreglar	to tidy, fix
averiguar	to check, to find out
ayudar	to help
bailar	to dance
bajar de	to get off (a bus)
beber	to drink
buscar	to look for
caer	to fall
cambiar	to change
cantar	to sing
cenar	to have dinner
cerrar	to close
coger	to take, to catch
comenzar	to start
comer	to eat
compartir	to share
comprar	to buy
conducir	to drive
conocer	to know (be familiar with)
contestar	to answer, reply
correr	to run
creer	to believe
cuidar	to look after
charlar	to chat

Verbs D–G

dar	to give
darse cuenta de	to realise
darse prisa	to hurry
deber	to have to, must
decir	to say
dejar	to leave (an object)
desayunar	to have breakfast
descargar (música)	to download (music)
desear	to wish
dibujar	to draw
dirigir	to manage, run, direct
discutir	to discuss, argue
disfrutar de	to enjoy
divertirse	to enjoy oneself
doler	to hurt
dormir	to sleep
ducharse	to shower
durar	to last
echar de menos (a)	to miss
elegir	to choose
empezar	to begin
encantar (a)	to love
encontrar	to find
enfadarse	to get angry
enseñar	to show, teach
entender	to understand
enviar	to send
equivocarse	to make a mistake
escribir	to write
escuchar	to listen
esperar	to hope, wait for
estar resfriado	to have a cold
estar	to be
evitar	to avoid
faltar	to be missing
ganar	to win, earn
gastar	to spend (money)
golpear	to hit
gustar (a)	to like

Verbs H–P

haber	to have (auxiliary verb)
hablar	to speak, talk
hacer	to do, make
ir de compras	to go shopping
ir	to go
lavar(se)	to wash (oneself)
leer	to read
levantarse	to get up
llamar	to call
llamarse	to be called
llegar	to arrive
llevar	to carry, wear
llevarse bien con	to get on well with
llorar	to cry
llover	to rain
jugar	to play
mandar	to send
montar (a caballo)	to ride (a horse)
morir	to die
nacer	to be born
nadar	to swim
navegar por Internet	to surf the internet
nevar	to snow
odiar	to hate
ofrecer (regalos)	to give (presents)
oír	to hear
olvidar	to forget
parar(se)	to stop
parecer	to seem
pasar	to spend (time)
pasear	to go for a walk
patinar	to skate
pedir	to ask (for)
pensar	to think
perder	to lose
poder	to be able to
poner	to put
preferir	to prefer
preguntar	to ask (a question)

Now try this

How accurate are your verbs? Pick three verbs from each column. For each verb, write out the full conjugation for the present, preterite and future tenses.

① High-frequency language

Verbs Q–V

quedarse	to stay, remain
quejarse	to complain
querer	to like, want
quitar la mesa	to clear the table
recordar	to remember
reembolsar	to refund
reír(se)	to laugh
rellenar (una ficha)	to fill out (a form)
repasar	to revise
robar	to steal
romper	to break
saber	to know (a fact)
sacar (buenas) notas	to get (good) marks
sacar entradas	to buy tickets
sacar fotos	to take photographs
salir	to leave
saltar	to jump
seguir	to follow, continue
sentarse	to sit down
ser	to be
sonreír	to smile
subir	to climb, go up
tener	to have
tener calor / frío	to be hot / cold
tener éxito	to be successful
tener hambre	to be hungry
tener prisa	to be in a hurry
tener que	to have to
tener sed	to be thirsty
tener sueño	to be sleepy, tired
tener suerte	to be lucky
tirar	to throw
tirar de	to pull
tocar	to play (a musical instrument)
tomar	to take
tomar el sol	to sunbathe
torcer	to twist
trabajar	to work
traer	to bring
tratar de	to try to
triunfar	to succeed
utilizar	to use
vender	to sell
venir	to come
ver	to see
vestirse	to get dressed
vivir	to live

Adjectives A–J

abierto/a	open
aburrido/a	bored, boring
activo/a	active
agradecido/a	grateful
alegre	happy, cheerful
alto/a	high, tall
amable	kind
anciano/a	(very) old
animado/a	lively
antiguo/a	former, old
antipático/a	unpleasant
asqueroso/a	disgusting
breve	brief
brillante	brilliant
bueno/a	good
buscado/a	sought after
caliente	hot
cansado/a	tired, tiring
castaño/a	chestnut brown
cercano/a	close
cerrado/a	closed
cómodo/a	comfortable
corto/a	short
de buen humor	in a good mood
débil	weak
delgado/a	thin
delicioso/a	delicious
deportista	sporty
difícil	difficult
divertido/a	amusing, fun
duro/a	hard
emocionante	exciting
enfadado/a	angry
entretenido/a	entertaining
estricto/a	strict
estupendo/a	great
entusiasmado/a	excited
fácil	easy
feo/a	ugly
fuerte	strong
gordo/a	fat
gran	great
grande	big, tall
gratis	free
guapo/a	handsome, pretty
guay	cool
hermoso/a	beautiful
horrible	awful
igual	same
increíble	unbelievable
joven	young
juntos/as	together

Adjectives L–V

largo/a	long
libre	free
ligero/a	light
limpio/a	clean
listo/a	ready, clever
lleno/a	full
maduro/a	mature
magnífico/a	magnificent
maravilloso/a	marvellous
mismo/a	same
necesario/a	necessary
numeroso/a	numerous
otro/a	other
pequeño/a	small
perdido/a	lost
perezoso/a	lazy
perfecto/a	perfect
pesado/a	heavy
podrido/a	rotten
preferido/a	favourite
propio/a	own
próximo/a	next
rápido/a	fast, quick
responsable	responsible
rico/a	rich, delicious
roto/a	broken
ruidoso/a	noisy
sabio/a	wise
sano/a	healthy
satisfecho/a	satisfied
sensacional	sensational
serio/a	serious
severo/a	strict
silencioso/a	silent
simpático/a	likeable, kind
solo/a	alone, lonely
sucio/a	dirty
tímido/a	shy
todo/a	all
tonto/a	silly
trabajador(a)	hardworking
tradicional	traditional
travieso/a	naughty
último/a	last, latest
útil	useful
válido/a	valid
valiente	brave
valioso/a	valuable
verdadero/a	true
viejo/a	old

Now try this

Choose 5 positive adjectives and 5 negative ones from this page. Write 10 sentences in Spanish using a different adjective in each.

Had a look ☐ Nearly there ☐ Nailed it! ☐

① High-frequency language

Adverbs

a menudo	often
a veces	sometimes
abajo	below (down)
afortunadamente	fortunately
ahí	over there
allí	there
aquí	here
arriba	up there
bastante	rather, quite
bien	well
casi	almost
demasiado	too
deprisa	quickly
desafortunadamente	unfortunately
desgraciadamente	unfortunately
durante mucho tiempo	for a long time
en seguida	straight away
especialmente	especially
inmediatamente	immediately
mal	badly
más	more
muy	very
otra vez	again
por suerte	luckily
quizás, quizá	perhaps
rápidamente	quickly
realmente	really
recientemente	recently
siempre	always
sobre todo	especially
todavía	still (yet)
ya	already

Connecting words

antes	before
aunque	though
después, luego	then, afterwards
entonces	then
lo primero (de todo)	first (of all)
o / u	or
pero	but
pues	then, since
sin embargo	however
también	also
y / e	and

Time expressions

a partir de	from
a tiempo	on time
ahora	now
ahora mismo	just now, straight away
al día siguiente	the next day
anoche	last night
anteayer	the day before yesterday
año (m)	year
año pasado	last year
ayer	yesterday
cada día	every day
de vez en cuando	from time to time
desde	since, from
día (m)	day
fin de semana (m)	weekend
hace	ago
hoy	today
luego	later
mañana	tomorrow
mañana (f)	morning
más tarde	later
noche (f)	night
pasado mañana	the day after tomorrow
pasado/a	last
por la mañana	in the morning
por la noche	at night
por la tarde	in the afternoon / evening
pronto	soon
próximo/a	next
puntual	on time
quince días	a fortnight
quincena (f)	a fortnight
semana (f)	week
siempre	always
siguiente	next
tarde (f)	afternoon, evening
temprano	early
todos los días	every day

Times

a la una	at one o'clock
a las dos	at two o'clock
a medianoche	at midnight
a mediodía	at noon
de la mañana	in the morning
de la noche	at night
de la tarde	in the afternoon / evening
es la una	it's one o'clock
hora (f)	hour
menos cuarto	quarter to
menos diez, etc.	ten to, etc.
minuto (m)	minute
son las dos, etc.	it's two o'clock, etc.
y cinco, etc.	five past, etc.
y cuarto	quarter past
y media	half past

Seasons

primavera (f)	spring
verano (m)	summer
otoño (m)	autumn
invierno (m)	winter

Colours

castaño/a	chestnut brown
claro/a	light
moreno/a	dark (hair, skin)
oscuro/a	dark
rubio/a	fair (hair, skin)
amarillo/a	
azul	
blanco/a	
gris	
marrón	
naranja	
negro/a	
rojo/a	
rosa	
verde	
violeta	

Son las dos y media

Son las tres menos cuarto

Now try this

Test yourself on the time expressions above by covering up the English column and then writing down the English translation yourself. Compare your answers with the list above. How many have you got right?

1 High-frequency language

Months of the year

enero	January
febrero	February
marzo	March
abril	April
mayo	May
junio	June
julio	July
agosto	August
septiembre	September
octubre	October
noviembre	November
diciembre	December

Days of the week

lunes	Monday
martes	Tuesday
miércoles	Wednesday
jueves	Thursday
viernes	Friday
sábado	Saturday
domingo	Sunday
el lunes	on Monday
los lunes	on Mondays
cada lunes	every Monday

Quantities

bastante	enough
exactamente	exactly
mucho/a/s	much, many
nada	nothing
solamente	only
suficiente	enough
un kilo de	a kilo of
un litro de	a litre of
un paquete de	a packet of
un trozo de	a piece of
un poco de	a little of
un tarro de	a jar of
un tercio de	a third of
una botella de	a bottle of
una caja de	a box of
una docena de	a dozen
una lata de	a tin of
una parte de	a part of
una rebanada de	a slice of
varios/as	several

Continents

África (f)	Africa
América del Norte (f)	North America
América del Sur (f)	South America
Asia (f)	Asia
Australia (f)	Australia
Europa (f)	Europe

Countries

Alemania (f)	Germany
Argentina (f)	Argentina
Austria (f)	Austria
Bélgica (f)	Belgium
Brasil (m)	Brazil
Dinamarca (f)	Denmark
Escocia (f)	Scotland
España (f)	Spain
Estados Unidos (mpl)	United States
Francia (f)	France
Gran Bretaña (f)	Great Britain
Grecia (f)	Greece
Holanda (f)	Holland
India (f)	India
Inglaterra (f)	England
Irlanda (f)	Ireland
Italia (f)	Italy
México (m)	Mexico
País de Gales (m)	Wales
Países Bajos (mpl)	Netherlands
Pakistán (m)	Pakistan
Perú (m)	Peru
Reino Unido (m)	United Kingdom
Rusia (f)	Russia
Suecia (f)	Sweden
Suiza (f)	Switzerland
Turquía (f)	Turkey

Nationalities

alemán/ana	German
americano/a	American
argentino/a	Argentinian
austríaco/a	Austrian
belga	Belgian
brasileño/a	Brazilian
británico/a	British
danés/esa	Danish
escocés/esa	Scottish
español(a)	Spanish
europeo/a	European
francés/esa	French
galés/esa	Welsh
griego/a	Greek
holandés/esa	Dutch
indio/a	Indian
inglés/esa	English
irlandés/esa	Irish
italiano/a	Italian
mexicano/a	Mexican
pakistaní	Pakistani
ruso/a	Russian
sueco/a	Swedish
suizo/a	Swiss
turco/a	Turkish
venezolano/a	Venezuelan

Now try this

Practise the days of the week and the months of the year by talking about the birthdays of family and friends in Spanish.

① High-frequency language

Prepositions

a	at, to
a causa de	because of
a través de	through
al final de	at the end of
al lado de	next to
alrededor de	around
antes de	before
cerca de	near
con	with
contra	against
de, desde	from
debajo de	under
delante de	in front of
dentro de	inside
después de	after
detrás de	behind
durante	during
en	in, on
en casa de	at (someone's house)
en la esquina de	on the corner of
encima de	above, on top
enfrente de	opposite
entre	between
excepto, salvo	except
fuera de	outside
hacia	towards
hasta	until
lejos de	far from
para	for
por	through, for
según	according to
sin	without
sobre	on

delante de in front of	detrás de behind

al lado de next to	entre between

cerca de near to	lejos de far from

Question words

¿Adónde?
Where to?

¿Cómo?
How?

¿Cuál?
Which?

¿Cuántos/as?
How many?

¿Dónde?
Where?

¿Para qué?
What for?

¿Cuándo?
When?

¿Cuánto?
How much?

¿Por qué?
Why?

¿Qué?
What?

¿Quién?
Who?

Social conventions

¿Diga?	hello (on the telephone)
adiós	goodbye
gracias	thank you
hasta luego	see you later
hasta mañana	see you tomorrow
hasta pronto	see you soon
hola	hi, hello
muchas gracias	thank you very much
por favor	please
¡Que te diviertas!	Enjoy yourself!
¡Que lo pases bien!	Have a good time!
saludos	best wishes
¡Socorro!	Help!

Other useful expressions

¿Cómo se escribe?	How do you spell that?
aquí (lo) tienes	here you are
bien	OK
buena suerte	good luck
con (mucho) gusto	with pleasure
depende	it depends
en mi opinión	in my opinion
estar a punto de	to be about to
(estoy) bien	I'm fine
he tenido bastante	I've had enough
me da igual	I don't mind
mío/a	mine
no importa (nada)	it doesn't matter
normalmente	usually
otra vez	once again
¡Qué lástima!	What a shame!
¡Qué pena!	What a shame!
por supuesto	of course

Now try this

Write a question in Spanish using each of the question words on this page.

② Identity and culture

Eating at home and in restaurants

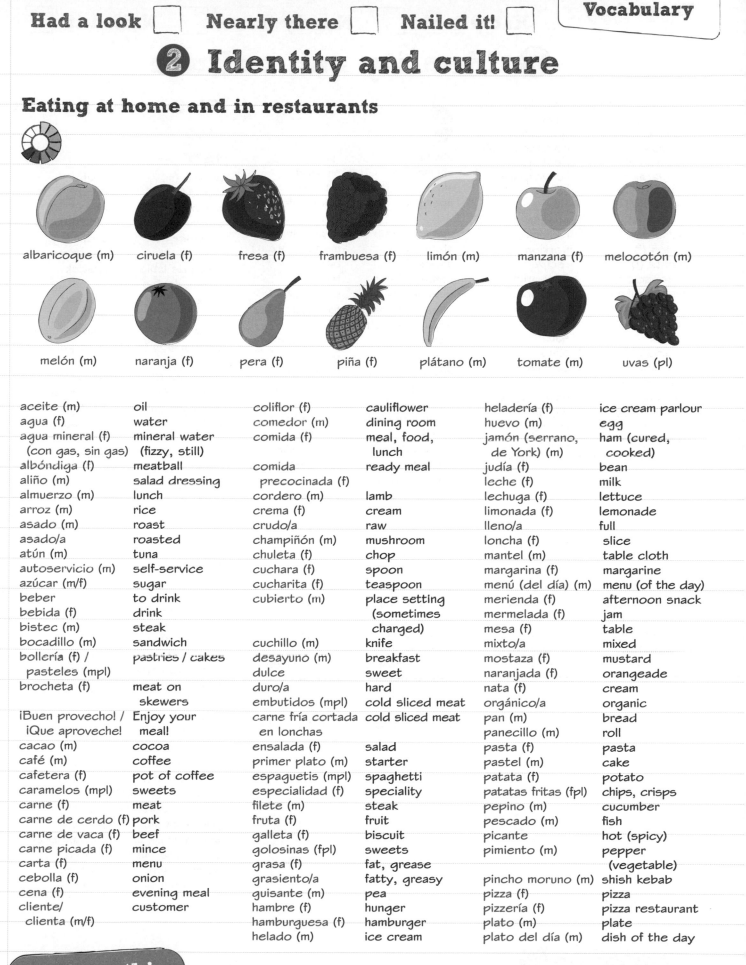

albaricoque (m)	ciruela (f)	fresa (f)	frambuesa (f)	limón (m)	manzana (f)	melocotón (m)
melón (m)	naranja (f)	pera (f)	piña (f)	plátano (m)	tomate (m)	uvas (pl)

aceite (m)	oil	coliflor (f)	cauliflower	heladería (f)	ice cream parlour
agua (f)	water	comedor (m)	dining room	huevo (m)	egg
agua mineral (f) (con gas, sin gas)	mineral water (fizzy, still)	comida (f)	meal, food, lunch	jamón (serrano, de York) (m)	ham (cured, cooked)
albóndiga (f)	meatball	comida precocinada (f)	ready meal	judía (f)	bean
aliño (m)	salad dressing			leche (f)	milk
almuerzo (m)	lunch	cordero (m)	lamb	lechuga (f)	lettuce
arroz (m)	rice	crema (f)	cream	limonada (f)	lemonade
asado (m)	roast	crudo/a	raw	lleno/a	full
asado/a	roasted	champiñón (m)	mushroom	loncha (f)	slice
atún (m)	tuna	chuleta (f)	chop	mantel (m)	table cloth
autoservicio (m)	self-service	cuchara (f)	spoon	margarina (f)	margarine
azúcar (m/f)	sugar	cucharita (f)	teaspoon	menú (del día) (m)	menu (of the day)
beber	to drink	cubierto (m)	place setting (sometimes charged)	merienda (f)	afternoon snack
bebida (f)	drink			mermelada (f)	jam
bistec (m)	steak			mesa (f)	table
bocadillo (m)	sandwich	cuchillo (m)	knife	mixto/a	mixed
bollería (f) / pasteles (mpl)	pastries / cakes	desayuno (m)	breakfast	mostaza (f)	mustard
		dulce	sweet	naranjada (f)	orangeade
brocheta (f)	meat on skewers	duro/a	hard	nata (f)	cream
		embutidos (mpl)	cold sliced meat	orgánico/a	organic
¡Buen provecho! / ¡Que aproveche!	Enjoy your meal!	carne fría cortada en lonchas	cold sliced meat	pan (m)	bread
				panecillo (m)	roll
cacao (m)	cocoa	ensalada (f)	salad	pasta (f)	pasta
café (m)	coffee	primer plato (m)	starter	pastel (m)	cake
cafetera (f)	pot of coffee	espaguetis (mpl)	spaghetti	patata (f)	potato
caramelos (mpl)	sweets	especialidad (f)	speciality	patatas fritas (fpl)	chips, crisps
carne (f)	meat	filete (m)	steak	pepino (m)	cucumber
carne de cerdo (f)	pork	fruta (f)	fruit	pescado (m)	fish
carne de vaca (f)	beef	galleta (f)	biscuit	picante	hot (spicy)
carne picada (f)	mince	golosinas (fpl)	sweets	pimiento (m)	pepper (vegetable)
carta (f)	menu	grasa (f)	fat, grease		
cebolla (f)	onion	grasiento/a	fatty, greasy	pincho moruno (m)	shish kebab
cena (f)	evening meal	guisante (m)	pea	pizza (f)	pizza
cliente/ clienta (m/f)	customer	hambre (f)	hunger	pizzería (f)	pizza restaurant
		hamburguesa (f)	hamburger	plato (m)	plate
		helado (m)	ice cream	plato del día (m)	dish of the day

Now try this

Make a list of all the food items you really like and a list of those you don't. Write an opinion sentence for each one. Can you justify your opinions too?

Me encanta el yogur porque es muy sabroso. Odio el atún porque no como pescado.

② Identity and culture

segundo plato (m)	main dish
pollo (m)	chicken
pomelo (m)	grapefruit
posada (f)	inn (traditional)
postre (m)	dessert
preparar	to prepare
probar	to try
propina (f)	tip
queso (m)	cheese
rábano (m)	radish
ración (f)	portion
receta (f)	recipe
refresco (m)	fizzy drink
restaurante (m)	restaurant
riquísimo/a	delicious
sabroso/a	tasty
sal (f)	salt
salado/a	salty
salchicha (f)	sausage
salón de té (m)	tea room
salsa (f)	sauce, gravy
servilleta (f)	napkin
seta (f)	mushroom
sopa (f)	soup
supermercado (m)	supermarket
tarro (m)	jar
tarta (f)	tart, cake
té (m)	tea
tenedor (m)	fork
tener hambre	to be hungry
tener sed	to be thirsty
tortilla (f)	omelette
tostada (f)	toast
vainilla (f)	vanilla
vegetariano/a	vegetarian
verduras (fpl)	vegetables
vinagre (m)	vinegar
vino (tinto, blanco) (m)	wine (red, white)
yogur (m)	yoghurt
zanahoria (f)	carrot
zumo (de fruta) (m)	(fruit) juice

ajo (m)	garlic
ahumado/a	smoked
alcachofa (f)	artichoke
aperitivo (m)	drink before a meal
apetitoso/a	appetising
al punto	medium (steak)
amargo/a	bitter
bandeja (f)	tray
bien hech/a	well-cooked
cerveza de barril (f)	(draught) beer
espinacas (fpl)	spinach
casero/a	homemade
ganso (m)	goose
huevo frito (m)	fried egg
huevo pasado por agua (m)	boiled egg
huevos revueltos (mpl)	scrambled eggs
leche entera (f)	full fat milk
leche (semi) desnatada (f)	(semi-)skimmed milk
mariscos (mpl)	seafood
miel (f)	honey
muy hecho	well done (steak)
pato (m)	duck
pavo (m)	turkey
picante	spicy
pistacho (m)	pistachio
platillo (m)	saucer
poco hecho	rare (steak)
puerros (mpl)	leeks
queso de cabra (m)	goat's cheese
salmón (m)	salmon
ternera (f)	veal
trucha (f)	trout
tisana / infusión (f)	fruit / herbal tea

Clothes and fashion

abrigo (m)	coat
algodón (m)	cotton
anillo (m)	ring
anticuado/a	old-fashioned
bañador (m)	swimming costume
barra de labios (f) / pintalabios (m)	lipstick
brazalete (m)	bracelet
botas (fpl)	boots
bragas (fpl)	pants, briefs
calzoncillos (mpl)	underpants
camisa (f)	shirt
camiseta (f)	T-shirt
camisón (m)	nightdress
cárdigan (m)	cardigan
collar (m)	necklace
corbata (f)	tie
de cuero	leather
de hilo	linen
de lana	wool
de lino	linen
de lunares	spotted
de rayas	striped
elegante	smart
estilo (m)	style
gorra (f)	cap
guante (m)	glove
holgado/a	loose
jersey (m)	jumper
joyas (fpl)	jewels
joyería (f)	jeweller's
leggings (mpl)	leggings
leotardos (mpl)	leggings
maquillaje (m)	make-up
marca (f)	make, brand
mediano/a	medium (size)
medias (fpl)	tights
número (m)	(shoe) size
pantalón (m), pantalones (mpl)	trousers
pantalón corto (m)	shorts
paraguas (m)	umbrella
pasado/a de moda	old-fashioned
pendiente (m)	earring
perfume (m)	perfume
pijama (m)	pyjamas

Now try this

Practise combining adjectives with an item of clothing – how would you translate 'a striped shirt'? You may need these in translations or role plays, so write down a list of 10 items now, then check your answers. Remember that the adjective or adjectival phrase will go after the item of clothing.

② Identity and culture

calcetín (m)

cinturón (m)

corbata (f)

Personal information, home life and relationships

zapato (m)

sombrero (m)

bufanda (f)

abuela (f)	grandmother
abuelita (f)	granny
abuelito (m)	grandpa
abuelo (m)	grandfather
abuelos (mpl)	grandparents
adolescente (m/f)	adolescent
adulto/a (m/f)	adult
simpático/a	likeable
amigo/a (m/f)	friend
amigo/a por correspondencia (m/f)	penfriend

polo (m)	polo shirt		
pulsera (f)	bracelet		
probador (m)	changing room		
pulóver (m)	jumper		
reloj (m)	watch	ajustado/a	tight
retro	retro	apretado/a	tight
ropa (f)	clothes	bata (f)	dressing gown
ropa de deporte (f)	sports kit	ceñido/a	tight
sostén (m)	bra	chaqueta de punto (f)	cardigan
sudadera (f)	sweatshirt		
suéter (m)	sweater	cortarse el pelo	to have one's hair cut
talla (f)	size		
tatuaje (m)	tattoo	de seda	silk
tienda de ropa (f)	clothes shop	de terciopelo	velvet
suelto/a	loose	maquillarse	to put on make-up
sujetador (m)	bra		
traje (m)	suit	modelo (m/f)	model
traje de baño (m)	swimsuit	peinarse	to comb one's hair, to have one's hair done
vaqueros (mpl)	jeans		
vestido (m)	dress		
vestir(se)	to dress		
vintage	vintage	pintarse	to put on make-up
zapatería (f)	shoe shop		
zapatillas de deporte (fpl)	trainers	sombrero de paja (m)	straw hat
		teñido/a	dyed
		zapatillas (fpl)	slippers

amistad (f)	friendship
amistoso/a	friendly
amor (m)	love
apartamento (m)	apartment
apellido (m)	surname
apodo (m)	nickname
arreglado/a	neat
ático (m)	loft
atrevido/a	adventurous
autoritario/a	bossy
avaro/a	mean
barba (f)	beard
barbudo/a	bearded
bebé (m)	baby
beso (m)	kiss
bigote (m)	moustache
bloque de pisos (m)	block of flats
boca (f)	mouth
boda (f)	wedding
butaca (f)	armchair
calvo/a	bald
cara (f)	face
carácter (m)	character
cariñoso/a	affectionate
casa (f)	house
casa adosada (f)	semi-detached / terraced house
casado/a	married
casamiento (m)	marriage, wedding
casarse (con)	to get married (to)
celebrar	to celebrate
celebridad (f)	celebrity
chica (f)	girl
chico (m)	boy

Now try this

Look at the clothes you and your friends are wearing today. Check you can translate them all into Spanish correctly.

② Identity and culture

perro (m)   conejo (m)   gato (m)   hámster (m)

pez de colores (m)   cobaya (f),   tortuga de tierra (f)
                           conejillo de Indias (m)

cocina (f)	kitchen	hermanos (mpl)	brothers, siblings	novia (f)	girlfriend, bride,
código postal (m)	postcode	guapo/a	beautiful		fiancée
comedor (m)	dining room	hija (f)	daughter	novio (m)	boyfriend,
cuadro (m)	painting	hijo (m)	son		groom, fiancé
cuarto de baño (m)	bathroom	hijo/a único/a	only child	nuera (f)	daughter-in-law
cumpleaños (m)	birthday	hogar (m)	home	ojos (mpl)	eyes
de buen /	in a good /	hombre (m)	man	optimista (m/f)	optimistic
mal humor	bad mood	humor (m)	mood	padre (m)	father
delgado/a	thin	ideal	ideal	padres (mpl)	parents
desagradable	nasty	inaguantable	unbearable	papá (m)	dad
desván (m)	loft	inteligente	intelligent	pelear(se)	to fight, argue
discutir	to argue	invitación (f)	invitation	persona (f)	person
divorciado/a	divorced	jardín (m)	garden	persona mayor (f)	grown-up
divorciarse	to divorce	juventud (f)	youth	personalidad (f)	personality
dormitorio (m)	bedroom	lacio/a	straight (hair)	pesimista (m/f)	pessimistic
edad (f)	age	liso/a	straight (hair)	piercing (m)	body piercing
egoísto/a	selfish	llevarse bien /	to get on well /	pintura (f)	painting
enamorado/a	in love	mal con	badly with	piso (m)	flat
encantador(a)	charming	lugar de	place of birth	primo/a (m/f)	cousin
esposa (f)	wife	nacimiento (m)		prometido/a	engaged
esposo (m)	husband	lugar de	place of	regalo (m)	present
estudio (m)	study	residencia (m)	residence	relación (f)	relationship
familia (f)	family	madre (f)	mother	reñir	to argue
famoso/a (m/f)	famous	malo/a	naughty	rizado/a	curly
fastidiar	to annoy	mamá (f)	mum	sala (de estar) (f)	living room
fecha de	date of birth	mandón/mandona	bossy	salón (m)	living room
nacimiento (f)		marido (m)	husband	sensibilidad (f)	feeling
felicidad (f)	happiness	matrimonio (m)	marriage	sentimiento (m)	feeling
flaco/a	thin	mayor	older	separado/a	separated
gafas (fpl)	glasses	el/la mayor (m/f)	the eldest	silla (f)	chair
garaje (m)	garage	miembro de la	family member	sillón (m)	armchair
gemelo/a	twin	familia (m)		sin sentido del	no sense of
gemelos (mpl)	twins	molestar	to annoy	humor	humour
gente (f)	people	muebles (mpl)	furniture	sobrina (f)	niece
hablador(a)	talkative	mujer (f)	woman, wife	sobrino (m)	nephew
hermana (f)	sister	multicultural	multicultural	solo/a	alone
hermanastra (f)	stepsister	nacido/a	born	tía (f)	aunt, woman/girl
hermanastro (m)	stepbrother	nieto/a (m/f)	grandchild	tío (m)	uncle, dude
hermano (m)	brother	niño/a (m/f)	child	tipo (m)	guy, bloke
		nombre de pila (m)	first name	tonto/a	silly, foolish
		normal	normal	vecino/a (m/f)	neighbour
				vida (f)	life
				yerno (m)	son-in-law

Now try this

To help you learn the vocabulary, copy out these words, classifying them in subtopics: family members, positive characteristics, negative characteristics, neutral characteristics, house and home.

② Identity and culture

buena acción (f)	good deed
acosar	to bully
adoptado/a	adopted
agradecer	to thank
amueblado/a	furnished
apoyar	to support
callado/a	quiet
característica (f)	character trait
celoso/a	jealous
compañero/a (m/f)	classmate
comprensivo/a	understanding
compromiso (m)	engagement
conocido/a (m/f)	acquaintance
dar las gracias a	to thank
de confianza	reliable
deprimido/a	depressed
discriminación (f)	discrimination
discusión (f)	argument
estar en desventaja	to be disadvantaged
experimentar	to experience
familiar (m)	relation
fe (f)	faith (religious)
fiel	faithful
grano (m)	spot, pimple
independiente	independent
intimidar	to bully
irritante	annoying
leal	loyal
loco/a	mad, crazy
madre soltera (f)	single mother
maleducado/a	rude
menor de edad	underage
mimado/a	spoilt
molesto/a	annoying
noviazgo (m)	engagement
novia (f)	fiancée, girlfriend
novio (m)	fiancé, boyfriend
padre soltero (m)	single father
pandilla (f)	gang
parecido/a	similar
pariente (m/f)	relative
pareja (f)	couple
pelea (f)	fight, argument
parecerse (a)	to resemble, look like
pretencioso/a	pretentious
racista (m/f)	racist
reunión (f)	meeting
responsable	reliable
riña (f)	argument

sensato/a	sensible
sensible	sensitive
sentido del humor (m)	sense of humour
soltero/a	single
sufrir	to suffer
tenaz	tenacious

Culture, hobbies and free time

actividad (f)	activity
afición (f)	hobby
ajedrez (m)	chess
alpinismo (m)	mountaineering
Año Nuevo (m)	New Year
asistir a	to attend (match etc.)
artes marciales (mpl)	martial arts
atletismo (m)	athletics
bádminton (m)	bádminton
bailar	to dance
baile (m)	dancing, dance
balón (m)	ball
baloncesto (m)	basketball
balonmano (m)	handball
grupo (m)	band
bicicleta de montaña (f)	mountain bike
boxeo (m)	boxing
cámara (f)	camera
salto en cama elástica (m)	trampolining
campo de deportes (m)	sports ground
cantante (m/f)	singer
CD (m)	CD
celebración (f)	celebration
ciclismo (m)	cycling
clásico/a	classical, classic
colección (f)	collection
coleccionar	to collect
concierto (m)	concert
concurso (m)	competition
consola de juegos (f)	games console
club (m)	club
club de jóvenes (m)	youth club
club nocturno (m)	nightclub
Cuaresma (f)	Lent
culebrón (m)	soap opera

deporte (m)	sport
deportes de alto riesgo (mpl)	extreme sports
deportes extremos (mpl)	extreme sports
día de la Madre (m)	Mother's Day
disco compacto (m)	CD
discoteca (f)	disco, nightclub
documental (m)	documentary
ejercitar(se)	to exercise
entrenar	to train
entretenimiento (m)	entertainment
Epifanía (f)	Twelfth Night, 6th January
equipo de música (m)	stereo system
equitación (f)	horse-riding
escalada (en roca) (f)	(rock) climbing
escenario (m)	stage
espectáculo (m)	show
esquí (m)	ski
esquí acuático (m)	water skiing
fanático/a de	fanatical about
felicitar	to congratulate
¡Feliz Año Nuevo!	Happy New Year!
¡Feliz cumpleaños!	Happy birthday!
fiesta (f)	party
(fisi)culturismo (m)	body building
fútbol (m)	football
gimnasia (f)	gymnastics
grupo (m)	group
hacer deporte	to do sport
hacer ejercicio	to exercise
hacer excursionismo	to ramble
hacer vela	to sail
historia de espías / de espionaje (f)	spy story
hockey (m)	hockey
jugar a los bolos	to go bowling (tenpin)
ir de caminata	to hike
ir de paseo	to go for a walk / stroll
ir de pesca	to go fishing
judo (m)	judo
juguete (m)	toy
jugador(a) (m/f)	player
juego (m)	game
kárate (m)	karate
lectura (f)	reading
libro (m)	book
Lunes de Pascua (m)	Easter Monday
máquina fotográfica (f)	camera

Now try this

To help you learn the vocabulary, make a list of the activities you enjoy doing and any that you dislike and create some opinion sentences. Remember to give reasons for these opinions!

② Identity and culture

marcar (un gol)	to score (a goal)
ir en monopatín (m)	skate boarding
montañismo (m)	mountaineering
móvil (m)	mobile phone
MP3	MP3 (file)
música (f)	music
música folklórica (f)	folk music
música pop (f)	pop music
nadar	to swim
natación (f)	swimming
Navidad (f)	Christmas
Nochebuena (f)	Christmas Eve
novela policíaca (f)	detective / police story
noticias (fpl)	news
obra de teatro (f)	play
ocio (m)	free time, leisure
orquesta (f)	orchestra
parapente (m)	paragliding
participar en	to participate in, to take part in
pasatiempo (m)	hobby
Pascua (f)	Easter
patinaje (m)	skating
patinar sobre ruedas	to roller-skate
película de aventuras (f)	adventure film
película de ciencia ficción (f)	science fiction film
película del Oeste (f)	Western (film)
película de fantasía (f)	fantasy film
película de terror (f)	horror film
película de misterio / suspense (f)	thriller (film)
película romántica / de amor (f)	romantic film
pelota (f)	ball
pescar	to fish
petanca (f)	boules, petanque (similar to bowls)

ping-pong (m)	table tennis
piragüismo (m)	canoeing
placer (m)	pleasure
programa de televisión (m)	TV programme
revista (f)	magazine
rugby (m)	rugby
romántico/a	romantic
sacar a pasear (al perro)	to take (the dog) for a walk
salón (m)	lounge
salto con paracaídas (m)	parachuting
ser miembro de	to be a member of
serie (f)	series
squash (m)	squash
surf/surfing (m)	surfing
tebeo (m)	comic
teclado (m)	keyboard
telenovela (f)	soap opera
tenis (m)	tennis
tenis de mesa (m)	table tennis
tiempo libre (m)	free time
vela (f)	sailing
videojuego (m)	video game
Viernes Santo (m)	Good Friday
voleibol (m)	volleyball

equipamiento deportivo (m)	sports equipment
audiencia (f)	audience
auriculares (mpl)	earphones
barco de vela (m)	sailing boat
bricolaje (m)	DIY
campeonato (m)	championship
caña de pescar (f)	fishing rod
comedia (f)	comedy
comedia musical (f)	musical comedy, musical
conocimiento (m)	knowledge
descanso (m)	half-time
división (f)	division (sports)
drama (m)	drama
esgrima (f)	fencing
juego de mesa (m)	board game
juego electrónico (m)	electronic game
liga (f)	league
mando a distancia (m)	remote control
medio tiempo (m)	half-time
melodía (f)	melody, tune

Toco (el / la) ...   I play (the) ...

violín (m)   guitarra (f)   trompeta (f)   flauta (f)

clarinete (m)   piano (m)   banjo (m)   batería (f)

Now try this

Write a list of the things you do in your free time and what your family members or friends do. For example:
Yo veo películas de terror y escucho música pop. Mi padre lee novelas policíacas.

② Identity and culture

película doblada (f)	dubbed film
película policíaca (f)	detective / police film
remo (m)	rowing
subtítulos (mpl)	subtitles
telespectador(a) (m/f)	viewer
televisión por cable (f)	cable TV
televisión por satélite (f)	satellite TV
tiro con arco (m)	archery
torneo (m)	tournament
velero (m)	sailing boat
versión original (subtitulada) (f)	original version (subtitled)
vestuarios (mpl)	changing rooms
videocámara (f)	video camera

Internet and social media

acoso cibernético (m)	cyber bullying
almacenar	to store
archivar	to file, save
barra oblicua (f)	forward slash
blog (m)	blog
borrar	to erase, delete
cámara web (f)	webcam
cargar	to load, upload
charlar en línea	to chat online
sala de chat (f)	chat room
chatear	to chat (online)
conexión (f)	connection
contraseña (de acceso) (f)	password
correo electrónico (m)	email
descargar	to download
digital	digital
disco (m)	disk
escribir a máquina	to type
grabar	to burn, record
guardar	to save, store
impresora (f)	printer
imprimir	to print
Internet (m)	internet
ordenador (m)	computer
página de Internet (f)	internet page
página de inicio (f)	homepage

página frontal (f)	homepage
página web (f)	webpage
pantalla (f)	screen
programador(a) (m/f)	programmer
quemar	to burn
ratón (m)	mouse
red social (f)	social network
riesgo (m)	risk
seguridad (f)	security
sitio web (f)	website
software (m)	software
sondeo (m)	survey
subir	to upload
tecla (f)	key (on keyboard)
teclado (m)	keyboard
virus (m)	virus
webcam (f)	webcam

archivo de datos (m)	data file
arroba (f)	@ (at)
base de datos (f)	database
correo web (m)	webmail
disco duro (m)	hard disk
enlace (m)	link
pantalla táctil (f)	touchscreen
procesador de textos (m)	word processor
subrayar	to underscore
tarjeta de memoria (f)	memory card

Now try this

Translate the following into Spanish:

1 I like to chat online with my friends in the evening.

2 Cyber bullying is not a problem at my school.

3 I want to be a programmer when I leave school.

❸ Local, national, international and global areas of interest

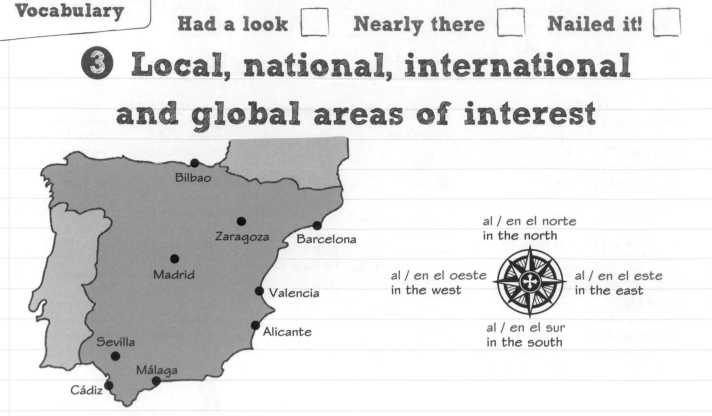

al / en el norte
in the north

al / en el oeste   al / en el este
in the west   in the east

al / en el sur
in the south

Bilbao está en el norte de España.

Visitor information

¡Que lo pases bien!	Enjoy your stay!	centro de la ciudad (m)	town centre	lago (m)	lake
abierto/a	open	cerrado/a	closed	lista de precios (f)	price list
acera (f)	pavement	cerveza de barril (f)	draught beer	lugar de interés (m)	place of interest
afueras (fpl)	outskirts	cita (f)	appointment	mapa de carreteras (m)	road map
al aire libre	in the open air	ciudad (f)	city	mar (m)	sea
al extranjero	abroad	colina (f)	hill	medios de comunicación (mpl)	media
aldea (f)	small village, hamlet	comunidad autónoma (f)	autonomous community	mercado (m)	market
alquilar	to rent	concierto (m)	concert	montaña (f)	mountain
alquiler de coches / bicicletas (m)	car / bike hire	control de pasaportes (m)	passport control	monumento (m)	monument
		corrida de toros (f)	bull fight	naturaleza (f)	nature
anuncio (m)	advertisement	costa (f)	coast	ocio (m)	leisure
apartamento (m)	apartment	descuento (m)	reduction	oficina de turismo (f)	tourist office
autopista (f)	motorway	día de fiesta (m)	public holiday		
barrio (m)	part of town	entrada (f)	entrance, admission	oficina de información turística (f)	tourist information office
bienvenido/a	welcome				
bosque (m)	wood	entretenimiento (m)	entertainment	país (m)	country
cafetería (f)	café	escaparate (m)	shop window	parque de atracciones (m)	amusement park
caja (f)	till, cash desk	estar situado/a	to be situated		
campo (m)	field, countryside	excursión (f)	tour	parte (f)	part (of town)
		exposición (f)	exhibition	peatón/ona (m/f)	pedestrian
capital (f)	capital city	extranjero/a (m/f)	foreigner	película (f)	film
carnet de identidad (m)	identity card	fiesta (f)	festival	periódico (m)	newspaper
		fiesta nacional (f)	public holiday	pintoresco/a	picturesque
cartel (m)	poster	folleto (m)	brochure / leaflet	piso (m)	flat
castillo (m)	castle	fuera	outside	plano (m)	map
catedral (f)	cathedral	habitante (m/f)	inhabitant	playa (f)	beach
		histórico/a	historic	plaza (f)	square
		horario de apertura (m)	opening hours	plaza de toros (f)	bull ring
				polución (f)	pollution
		industrial	industrial	postal (f)	postcard
		isla (f)	island	póster (m)	poster

Now try this

Pick out 10–15 words from this page that you could use to describe a recent trip or holiday. Memorise them, then try to write a short sentence with each.

❸ Local, national, international and global areas of interest

precio de entrada (m)	entry fee
prensa (f)	press
prohibido/a	forbidden
provincia (f)	province
público/a	public
pueblo (m)	town
recorrido (m)	tour
recuerdo (m)	souvenir
región (f)	region
reservar	to book
río (m)	river
salida (f)	exit
selva tropical (f)	rainforest
señal (f)	sign
sitio (m)	place
suburbio (m)	suburb
tarjeta telefónica (f)	telephone card
torre (f)	tower
tranquilo/a	quiet
turista (m/f)	tourist
vale la pena ver	well worth seeing
vida nocturna (f)	nightlife
visita (f)	visit
visita guiada a pie (f)	walking tour
zona (f)	part of town
zona peatonal (f)	pedestrian area
zona residencial (f)	suburb
zona verde (f)	park, green space

acontecimiento (m)	event
aduana (f)	customs
alrededores (mpl)	surrounding area
canal (m)	canal
centro turístico costero (m)	seaside resort
centro de la ciudad (m)	town centre
desfile (m)	procession
estancia (f)	stay
experiencia (f)	experience
fuegos artificiales (mpl)	fireworks
fuente (f)	fountain
hospitalidad (f)	hospitality

memoria (f)	memory
rastro (m)	fleamarket
recuerdo (m)	souvenir
salida de emergencia (f)	emergency exit
suceso (m)	event
tener lugar	to take place
vacaciones de esquí (fpl)	skiing holiday
vacaciones de invierno (fpl)	winter holiday
viaje organizado (m)	package holiday

Facilities

abierto/a	open
aeropuerto (m)	airport
aseos (mpl)	toilets
ayuntamiento (m)	town hall
banco (m)	bank
banco (m)	seat, bench
biblioteca (f)	library
bloque de pisos (m)	tower block
bolera (f)	bowling alley (tenpin)
café (m)	café
cafetería (f)	café
cancha de tenis (f)	tennis court
carnicería (f)	butcher's
castillo (m)	castle
catedral (f)	cathedral
centro comercial (m)	shopping centre
centro de ocio (m)	leisure centre
cerrado/a	closed
cine (m)	cinema
clínica (f)	hospital, clinic
comercio (m)	business
comisaría (f)	police station
Correos (mpl)	Post Office
cubo de basura (m)	rubbish bin
discoteca (f)	disco, nightclub
edificio (m)	building
estación de autobuses (f)	bus station
estación de tren (f)	railway station
estación de servicio (f)	service station
estadio (m)	stadium
fábrica (f)	factory
farmacia (f)	chemist's

frutería (f)	fruit shop
galería de arte (f)	art gallery
gasolinera (f)	petrol station
grandes almacenes (mpl)	department store
granja (f)	farm
hospital (m)	hospital
iglesia (f)	church
industria (f)	industry
lavandería (automática) (f)	laundry (launderette)
librería (f)	book shop
mercado (m)	market
municipal	public, municipal
museo (m)	museum
negocio (m)	business
oficina de correos (f)	post office
palacio (m)	palace
parque (m)	park
patio (de recreo) (m)	playground
pescadería (f)	fishmonger's
piscina (cubierta) (f)	(indoor) pool
pista de (patinaje sobre) hielo (f)	ice rink
policía (m/f)	police officer
policía (m/f) / guardia civil (m/f)	policeman/ woman
polideportivo (m)	leisure centre
puente (m)	bridge
puerto (m)	port
quiosco (m)	newspaper stall
servicios (mpl)	toilets
supermercado (m)	supermarket
teatro (m)	theatre
tienda (f)	shop
tienda de comestibles (f)	grocer's

caja de ahorros (f)	savings bank
cajero automático (m)	cashpoint, ATM
ferretería (f)	hardware shop
limpieza en seco (f)	dry cleaning
parque zoológico / zoo (m)	zoo
tintorería (f)	dry cleaner's
torre de pisos (f)	tower block

Now try this

Think about a place you have been on holiday or somewhere you would like to go. Make a list of the facilities and types of accommodation it has.

❸ Local, national, international and global areas of interest

Accommodation

acampar	to camp
agua potable (f)	drinking water
albergue juvenil (m)	youth hostel
alojamiento (m)	accommodation
alquería (f)	farm house
alquilar	to hire, rent
almohada (f)	pillow
amueblado/a	furnished
apagar	to turn / switch off
armario (m)	wardrobe
ascensor (m)	lift
balcón (m)	balcony
bañera (f)	bath tub
baño (m)	bathroom
calefacción (f)	heating
cama (f)	bed
camping (m)	campsite
caravana (f)	caravan
cepillo de dientes (m)	toothbrush
colonia de vacaciones (f)	holiday camp
colonia de verano (f)	summer camp
cuarto de baño (m)	bathroom
deshacer la maleta	to unpack
ducha (f)	shower
dueño/a (m/f)	owner
en el campo	in the country
en el primer piso	on the first floor
encender	to turn / switch on
equipaje (m)	luggage
escalera (f)	staircase
formulario (m)	form
funcionar	to work
garaje (m)	garage
habitación con dos camas (f)	twin room
habitación doble (f)	double room
habitación individual (f)	single room
hotel (m)	hotel
incluido/a	included
jabón (m)	soap

jardín (m)	garden
lavabo (m)	wash basin
libre	vacant
litera (f)	bunk bed
llave (f)	key
llegada (f)	arrival
maleta (f)	suitcase
media pensión (f)	half-board
ocupado/a	occupied
papel higiénico (m)	toilet paper
pasta de dientes (f)	toothpaste
pensión (f)	guest house
pensión completa (f)	full board
piso (m)	floor, flat
planta (f)	floor
planta baja (f)	ground floor
puerta (principal) (f)	(front) door
recepción (f)	reception
recepcionista (m/f)	receptionist
ropa de cama (f)	bed linen
sábana (f)	sheet
saco de dormir (m)	sleeping bag
sala de juegos (f)	games room
salida (f)	exit
salón (m)	lounge
segundo/a	second
sótano (m)	basement
suelo (m)	floor
suplemento (m)	supplement
tienda (de campaña) (f)	tent
toalla de baño (f)	bath towel
ventana (f)	window
vista (f)	view

aire acondicionado (m)	air conditioning
alojamiento (m)	accomodation
alojarse	to stay
confirmar	to confirm
registro (m)	registration / booking in
ruido (m)	noise
salida de emergencia (f)	emergency exit

Transport

a pie	on foot
aeropuerto (m)	airport
andén (m)	platform
aparcamiento (m)	car park
asiento (m)	seat
atasco (m)	traffic jam
autobús (m)	bus
autocar (m)	coach
autopista (f)	motorway
autovía (f)	main road
avión (m)	plane
barco (m)	boat
bici (f)	bike
billete (m)	ticket
calle (f)	street
camino (m)	way, road
camión (m)	lorry
carretera (f)	road
ciclomotor (m)	moped
circulación (f)	traffic
coche (m)	car
coche-cama (m)	sleeping car
compartimento (m)	compartment
conductor(a) (m/f)	driver
conexión (f)	connection
consigna (f)	left luggage
cruce (m)	crossroads
de ida	single
de ida y vuelta	return
de segunda clase	second class
descuento (m)	reduction
despegar	to take off (plane)
desvío (m)	detour
dirección (f)	direction
dirección única (f)	one-way street
directo/a	direct
enlace (m)	connection
estación de autobuses (f)	bus / coach station
ferry (m)	ferry
gasoil (m)	diesel
gasolina (f)	petrol
horario (m)	timetable
línea (f)	line / route

Now try this

Imagine you go on holiday and travel somewhere on public transport, but it is the journey from hell! Write some sentences to describe what happened.

3 Local, national, international and global areas of interest

medio de transporte (m)	means of transport
taquilla (f)	ticket office
moto (f)	motorbike
ocupado/a	occupied / taken
parada (f)	bus stop
pasajero/a (m/f)	passenger
paso de peatones (m)	pedestrian crossing
perder	to miss (train, etc.)
permiso/carnet de conducir (m)	driving licence
por adelantado	in advance
prioridad (a la derecha) (f)	priority (to the right)
puerto (m)	port
rotunda (f)	roundabout
retraso (m)	delay
revisor(a) (m/f)	ticket inspector
sala de espera (f)	waiting room
salida (f)	departure, exit
semáforo (m)	traffic lights
señal (f)	sign
sentido (m)	direction
sentido único (m)	one-way system
sin plomo	unleaded
taxi (m)	taxi
tranvía (m)	tram
tren (m)	train
validar	to validate (a ticket)
vía (f)	platform, track
viaje (m)	journey

adelantar	to overtake
atropellar	to run over
cinturón de seguridad (m)	seatbelt
embarcar	to board, embark
frenar	to brake
helicóptero (m)	helicopter

hora punta (f)	rush hour
límite de velocidad (m)	speed limit
pasaje a nivel (m)	level crossing
peaje (m)	toll
prohibido aparcar	no parking
salida de autopista (f)	motorway junction
salida de emergencia (f)	emergency exit
vehículo de gran tonelaje (m)	heavy goods vehicle

Directions

a la derecha	on the right
a la izquierda	on the left
atravesar	to cross
de cerca	near
cruzar	to cross
doblar	to turn
está a 100 metros	it's 100 metres away
estar situado/a	to be situated
esquina (f)	corner
hasta	as far as
la primera a la derecha	the first on the right
la segunda a la izquierda	the second on the left
lejos	far
seguir todo recto	to go straight on
tomar	to take

Holiday problems

accidente (m)	accident
asegurar	to insure
avería (f)	breakdown
billetero (m)	wallet
cambiar	to exchange, replace
cantidad (f)	quantity
cartera (f)	wallet
colisión (f)	collision
daño (m)	damage
defecto (m)	fault
descuento (m)	reduction, discount
devolver	to give back
dirección (f)	address
entrega (f)	delivery
entregar	to deliver
error (m)	mistake
factura (f)	bill
formulario (m)	form
garantía (f)	guarantee
garantizar	to guarantee
hacer reparto(s)	to deliver
(servicio de) información y reclamaciones	customer service
monedero (m)	purse
piezas de recambio (fpl)	replacement parts
pagar	to pay
queja (f)	complaint
quejarse	to complain
rebaja (f)	reduction
recibo (m)	receipt
reemplazar	to replace
reparar	to repair
robo (m)	theft
roto/a	broken
seguro (m)	insurance
volver	to return

Now try this

Choose two places you know well which you can walk or drive to in 5-10 minutes. Now describe the route in Spanish. Make sure you include as many details as possible to make it easy for someone to follow. Use the following instructions: 'toma' for 'take', 'dobla' for 'turn' and 'cruza' for 'cross'.

3 Local, national, international and global areas of interest

Weather

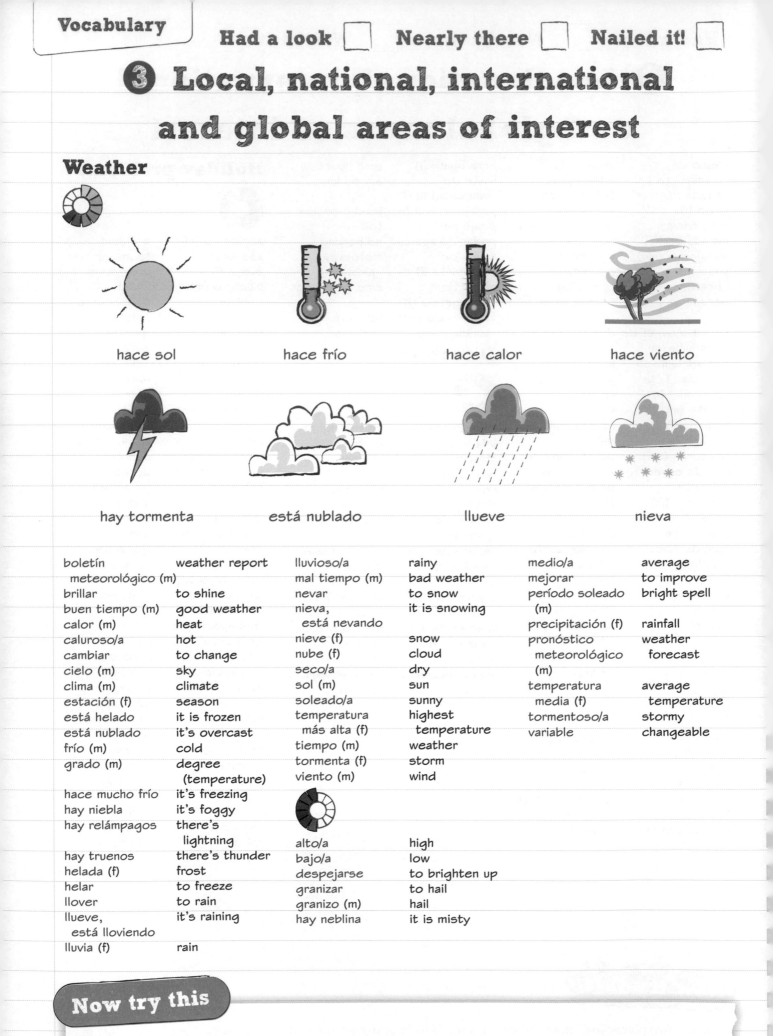

hace sol   hace frío   hace calor   hace viento

hay tormenta   está nublado   llueve   nieva

boletín meteorológico (m)	weather report	lluvioso/a	rainy
brillar	to shine	mal tiempo (m)	bad weather
buen tiempo (m)	good weather	nevar	to snow
calor (m)	heat	nieva, está nevando	it is snowing
caluroso/a	hot	nieve (f)	snow
cambiar	to change	nube (f)	cloud
cielo (m)	sky	seco/a	dry
clima (m)	climate	sol (m)	sun
estación (f)	season	soleado/a	sunny
está helado	it is frozen	temperatura más alta (f)	highest temperature
está nublado	it's overcast	tiempo (m)	weather
frío (m)	cold	tormenta (f)	storm
grado (m)	degree (temperature)	viento (m)	wind
hace mucho frío	it's freezing		
hay niebla	it's foggy		
hay relámpagos	there's lightning	alto/a	high
hay truenos	there's thunder	bajo/a	low
helada (f)	frost	despejarse	to brighten up
helar	to freeze	granizar	to hail
llover	to rain	granizo (m)	hail
llueve, está lloviendo	it's raining	hay neblina	it is misty
lluvia (f)	rain		

medio/a	average
mejorar	to improve
período soleado (m)	bright spell
precipitación (f)	rainfall
pronóstico meteorológico (m)	weather forecast
temperatura media (f)	average temperature
tormentoso/a	stormy
variable	changeable

Now try this

Close your book and write down as many weather expressions as you can in one minute. Then check here to see which ones you did not remember.

3 Local, national, international and global areas of interest

Global issues

agua potable (f)	drinking water
medio ambiente (m)	environment
animales (mpl)	animals
basura (f)	rubbish
beneficiencia (f)	charity
campaña (f)	campaign
campo (m)	country(side)
carbón (m)	coal
comercio justo (m)	fair trade
contaminación (f)	pollution
contra	against
derechos (mpl)	rights
desastre (m)	disaster
desigualdad (f)	inequality
desventajas (fpl)	disadvantages
electricidad (f)	electricity
energía (f)	energy, power
falta (de) (f)	lack (of)
gas (m)	gas
gente (f)	people
global	global
gobierno (m)	government
grave	serious
guerra (f)	war
hambre (f)	hunger
huracán (m)	hurricane
igualdad (f)	equality
inquietante	alarming
internacional	international
inundaciones (fpl)	flooding, floods
Juegos Olímpicos (mpl)	Olympic Games
mundial (m)	world cup (football)
mundo (m)	world
morir	to die
país (m)	country
petróleo (m)	oil
planeta (m)	planet
pobreza (f)	poverty
polución (f)	pollution

por	for
preocupante	worrying
protección (f)	protection
proteger	to protect
reciclaje (m)	recycling
reciclar	to recycle
recursos naturales (mpl)	natural resources
selva tropical (f)	rainforest
sequía (f)	drought
tierra (f)	earth
ventaja (f)	advantage
vivir	to live

agua dulce (f)	freshwater
agua salada (f)	saltwater
amenazar	to threaten
aprovechar	to make the most of
arruinar	to ruin
aumento (de) (m)	increase (in)
calentamiento global (m)	global warming
climático/a	climatic
combatir	to fight, combat
contaminar	to contaminate, pollute
convertir en abono	to (make into) compost
cuidar	to save, keep safe
derechos (mpl)	rights
echar la culpa a	to put the blame on
energía solar (f)	solar power
escasez (de) (f)	shortage (of)
especie (f)	species
espiando	spying
faltar	to be lacking
inmediato/a	instant
mantener el contacto	to stay in contact
necesitado/a	unfortunate, needy

prejuicio (m)	prejudice
seguridad (f)	security
separar	to sort / separate
'sin techo' (mpl)	homeless people
sobrevivir	to survive
terremoto (m)	earthquake
ventajas (fpl)	advantages
volcán (m)	volcano

Now try this

Write ten recommendations for looking after the environment using *Debemos* (we must) or No debemos (we must not) followed by an infinitive and then a noun. For example:

- *Debemos proteger los animales.*
- *No debemos arruinar el paisaje.*

④ Current and future study and employment

Life at school

adecuado/a	satisfactory
alemán (m)	German
alumno/a (m/f)	pupil
año escolar / académico (m)	school year
aprobar (un examen)	to pass (an exam)
arte (m)	art
arte dramático (m)	drama
asignatura (f)	subject
aula (f)	classroom
ausente	absent
autobús escolar (m)	school bus
bachillerato (m)	equivalent of A levels
biblioteca (f)	library
biología (f)	biology
bloc de notas (m)	pad of paper
boletín de notas (m)	school report
bolígrafo, boli (m)	ballpoint pen
calculadora (f)	calculator
calificación (f)	qualification, mark
campo de deportes (m)	sports field
cantina (f)	canteen
castigo (m)	detention
ciclomotor (m)	moped
ciencias (fpl)	sciences
clase (f)	classroom, lesson
cocina (f)	food technology
colegio privado (m)	private school
conserje (m/f)	caretaker
contestar	to answer
continuar con	to continue with
copiar	to copy
corbata (f)	tie
coro (m)	choir
corregir	to correct
cuaderno (m)	exercise book
deberes (mpl)	homework
débil	weak
desarrollo (m)	progress
descanso para comer (m)	lunch break
despacho (m)	office
dibujo (m)	art
diccionario (m)	dictionary
director(a) (m/f)	headteacher
discutir	to discuss, argue

diseño (m)	DT
durar	to last
educación física (f)	PE
educación personal, social y sanitaria (f)	PSE, PSHE
Educación Secundaria Obligatoria (f)	GCSE equivalent
ejercicio (m)	exercise
enseñar	to teach
equipo (m)	team
escrito/a	written
escuela primaria (f)	primary school
escuela pública (f)	state school
español (m)	Spanish
estado (m)	state
estricto/a	strict
estuche (m)	pencil case
estudiante (m/f)	student
estudiar	to study
evaluación (f)	test
examen (m)	examination
excursión del instituto (f)	school trip
éxito (m)	success
experimento (m)	experiment
física (f)	physics
flojo/a en	weak, bad at (subject)
francés (m)	French
fuerte en	good at (subject)
geografía (f)	geography
gimnasia (f)	gymnastics
gimnasio (m)	gym
goma (f)	rubber
hacer un examen	to sit an exam
historia (f)	history
hoja de ejercicios (f)	worksheet
hoja de examen (f)	exam paper
horario (m)	timetable
humanidades (fpl)	humanities
idioma (m)	foreign (language)
inadecuado/a	inadequate
informática (f)	ICT
inglés (m)	English
injusto/a	unfair
instituto (de educación secundaria) (m)	secondary school
instituto para alumnos de 16 a 18 años (m)	sixth form college
intercambio (m)	exchange

italiano (m)	Italian
jornada escolar (f)	school day
justo/a	fair
laboratorio (m)	laboratory
laboratorio de idiomas (m)	language lab
lápiz (m)	pencil
latín (m)	Latin
lengua (f)	language
lenguas extranjeras (fpl)	foreign languages
libro de texto (escolar) (m)	school book
listo/a	clever
mochila (f)	school bag
matemáticas (fpl)	maths
materia (f)	school subject
mixto/a	mixed
música (f)	music
muy buena nota (f)	very good mark
norma (f)	rule
orientador(a) (m/f)	careers adviser
orientación profesional (f)	careers advice
página (f)	page
parvulario (m)	nursery school
pasillo (m)	corridor
patio de recreo (m)	playground
pegamento (m)	glue
perezoso/a	lazy
periódico del instituto (m)	school newspaper
periodismo (m)	media studies, journalism
pizarra (f)	board
planes para el futuro (mpl)	future plans
pluma (estilográfica) (f)	(fountain) pen
polideportivo (m)	sports hall
práctica (f)	exercise
practicar	to practise
pregunta (f)	question
preescolar (m)	pre-school
prestar atención	to pay attention
progreso (m)	progress
proyector (m)	projector
prueba (f)	class test
pupitre (m)	desk
química (f)	chemistry
(re)llenar	to fill out
recreo (m)	break time
regla (f)	ruler
religión (f)	RE, religion
rendimiento (m)	performance
repasar	to revise
reportaje (m)	report

Now try this

Can you list all the subjects you are studying and spell them correctly? Can you also write down the facilities that your school has?

④ Current and future study and employment

respuesta (f)	answer			lector(a) (m/f)	foreign language assistant
reunión (f)	assembly			libro de texto (m)	text book
rotulador (m)	felt-tip pen			licenciatura (f)	degree (university)
sacapuntas (m)	sharpener				
sala de profesores (f)	staff room	a distancia	distance (learning)	mejorar	to improve
		auriculares (mpl)	headphones	optativo/a	optional
seguir	to continue	auxiliar de lengua (m/f)	foreign language assistant	pasar lista (f)	to take the register
semestre (m)	semester				
sociología (f)	sociology	cartucho de tinta (m)	ink cartridge	pasar de curso	to move up (a year)
suspender (un examen)	to fail (an exam)	centro de capacitación (m)	training centre	pérdida de tiempo (f)	waste of time
tarea (f)	task				
tecnología (f)	technology / DT	conocimiento (m)	knowledge	permiso (m)	permission
tecnología de alimentos (f)	food technology	dejar	to drop (a subject)	presión (f)	pressure (to do well)
tener cuidado	to be careful	deletrear	to spell		
tijeras (fpl)	scissors	derecho (m)	law	pronunciación (f)	pronunciation (parents')
título (m)	qualification	dotado/a	gifted	reunión (de padres) (f)	meeting
trabajador/a	hardworking	economía (f)	economics		
trimestre (m)	term	estar castigado/a	to have a detention	se ha cancelado	has been cancelled
uniforme (m)	uniform				
universidad (f)	university	estar de acuerdo con	to agree with	título (m)	degree (university)
vacaciones de mitad de trimestre (fpl)	half-term	estudios (mpl)	studies	trabajo (m)	essay
		examen de fin de curso (m)	end of year exam	traducción (f)	translation
vacaciones de verano (fpl)	summer holidays	explicar	to explain		
salón de actos del colegio/del instituto (f)	school hall	habilidades (fpl)	skills		
		hacer novillos	to play truant		
vestuario (m)	changing room	internado (m)	boarding school		
vuelta al instituto (m)	first day back at school	hacer un castigo escrito	to do a written punishment, lines		

Now try this

List three things you plan to do after your exams and explain why you want to do them. Then write three sentences about things you won't do and why.

④ Current and future study and employment

actor (m)	actor
actriz (f)	actress
agencia de viajes (f)	travel agency
agente de policía (m/f)	police officer
agricultor(a) (m/f)	farmer
albañil (m)	builder
ambición (f)	ambition
anuncio (m)	advertisment
aprendizaje (m)	apprenticeship
archivo (m)	file
archivar	to file
arquitecto/a (m/f)	architect
artista (m/f)	artist
azafato/a (m/f)	air steward(ess)
beneficiencia (f)	charity
bien pagado/a	well paid
cajero/a (m/f)	cashier
camarero/a (m/f)	waiter / waitress
carnicero/a (m/f)	butcher
carpeta (f)	folder
cocinero/a (m/f)	chef, cook
colega (m/f)	colleague
colgar	to hang up
comercio (m)	business
como voluntario/a (m/f)	as a volunteer
compañía (f)	company
concurrido/a	busy (place)
condiciones de empleo (mpl)	terms of employment
conductor(a) (m/f)	driver
con experiencia	with experience
conferencia (f)	conference
contestador automático (m)	answering machine
costura (f)	sewing
dentista (m/f)	dentist
desempleado/a	unemployed
director(a) (m/f)	manager
diseñador(a) (m/f)	designer
educativo/a	educational
electricista (m/f)	electrician
empleado/a (m/f)	employee
empleo (m)	job
empresa (f)	company
empresario/a (m/f)	employer
en el extranjero	abroad
enfermero/a (m/f)	nurse
entrevista de trabajo (f)	job interview
esfuerzo (m)	work, effort
estar en paro	to be unemployed
estudiante (m/f)	student
expediente (m)	file
experiencia laboral (f)	work experience
farmacéutico/a (m/f)	pharmacist
fontanero/a (m/f)	plumber
formación (f)	training
funcionario/a (m/f)	civil servant
granjero/a (m/f)	farmer
hacer un curso	to do a course
informático/a (m/f)	computer scientist
ingeniero/a (m/f)	engineer
formación profesional (f)	vocational training
lenguaje (m)	language
llamada telefónica (f)	telephone call
mal pagado/a	badly paid
marcar el número	to dial the number
mecánico/a (m/f)	mechanic
médico/a (m/f)	doctor
mensaje (m)	message
mercadotecnia (f) / marketing (m)	marketing
moda (f)	fashion
músico/a (m/f)	musician
negocio (m)	business
ocupado/a	busy
panadero/a	baker
pastelero/a (m/f)	baker, cake maker
periodista (m/f)	journalist
planificado/a	planned
poeta (m/f)	poet
por hora	per hour
prácticas laborables (f)	work experience
profesor(a) (m/f)	teacher
programador(a) (m/f)	programmer
rellenar un formulario	to fill in a form
representante de ventas (m/f)	sales rep
reunión (f)	meeting
salario (m)	salary
sastrería (f)	tailoring
sin cobrar	without pay
solicitar un trabajo	to apply for a job
sueldo (m)	salary
sueño (m)	dream
técnico/a (m/f)	technician
a tiempo parcial	part time
tienda (f)	shop
trabajador(a) agrícola (m/f)	farmworker
trabajo (m)	job
una organización benéfica (f)	a charity
universidad (f)	university
voluntariamente	voluntarily
adjuntar	to enclose
adjunto/a	enclosed, attached
aprendiz (m/f)	apprentice
ascenso (m)	promotion
titulado/a	qualified
carta de presentación (f)	letter of application
cita (f)	appointment
en beneficio de	in aid of
enseñanza superior (f)	higher education
enviar	to send
firma (f)	signature
impresión (f)	impression
incluir	to enclose
inscribirse	to enrol, apply
ley (f)	law
mandar	to send
matricularse	to enrol
medicina (f)	medicine
meta (f)	goal
objetivo (m)	objective
ocupación (f)	occupation
oficio (m)	job
posibilidades de promoción (fpl)	promotion prospects
posición (f)	position
prácticas (fpl)	internship
presentarse	to introduce oneself
profesión (f)	profession
propósito (m)	aim
rellenar	to fill in
solicitar en	to apply at
solicitar un puesto de trabajo	to apply for a job
solicitud (f)	application form
titulado/a	qualified
título (m)	qualification
vacante (m)	vacancy
venta benéfica (f)	charity sale

Now try this

Write down a list of four people in your family or friends who work.
Now write down notes in Spanish, next to their names:
• What job they do   • Whether they like it and why
Finally write a sentence in Spanish from your notes about each person.

ANSWERS

Identity and culture

1. Physical descriptions

(a) A, (b) D, (c) C, (d) B, (e) A

2. Character descriptions

Sample answer
En mi opinión, soy bastante sensato y creo que también soy muy amistoso. No obstante, no estoy muy seguro de mí mismo y puedo ser un poco tímido. Cuando era pequeño, era muy travieso y un poco avaro con mis hermanos.

3. Describing family

B

4. Friends

Sample answer
En mi opinión, los amigos están ahí para apoyarte; no siempre están a tu lado pero pueden guardar tus secretos. Deben aceptarte como eres. Creo que los amigos son tan importantes como la familia. Es esencial que los amigos se lleven bien. A mi parecer, la amistad es más importante que el amor.

5. Relationships

(a) 15 years old
(b) He married his former fiancée's cousin
(c) 2 years before
(d) The identity of the former fiancé/boyfriend

7. When I was younger

(a) They used to climb big trees in the garden.
(b) They used to watch their favourite programmes on TV.

8. Social Media

B

9. Technology

(a) G, (b) G, (c) P, (d) P+G, (e) G

10. The internet

Sample answer
Normalmente compro por Internet porque es barato y bastante fácil. En casa, mis padres suelen enviar y recibir correos electrónicos pero mi hermana y yo leemos páginas web y utilizamos las salas de chat. El año pasado me compré un móvil nuevo por Internet y no fue difícil. Mañana voy a navegar por Internet para buscar unos videojuegos.

11. Pros and cons of technology

B, C, F

12. Hobbies

(a) D, (b) A, (c) B

13. Music

Sample answer
A mí me encanta la música y ahora estoy aprendiendo a tocar la flauta. Antes tocaba la guitarra pero después de ir a un concierto de música clásica con mis padres, decidí aprender a tocar la flauta. Es un instrumento que tiene un sonido suave y bonito. En el futuro tengo la intención de tocar en la orquesta del instituto porque me encanta participar en conciertos con otra gente.

14. Music events

Sample answer
C = candidate, T = teacher
T: ¿Qué hay en la foto?
C: En esta foto la gente está en un estadio escuchando un concierto de música rock. Hay muchos espectadores y el escenario es bastante grande.
T: ¿Te gustan los conciertos de música? ¿Por qué (no)?
C: Me encantan los conciertos. Creo que el ambiente es fenomenal y es emocionante estar con muchas otras personas que tienen los mismos gustos musicales.
T: ¿Cómo fue el último concierto que viste?
C: Mis amigos y yo fuimos a un concierto de nuestro grupo favorito. Bailamos mucho porque conocíamos todas las canciones. Fue una experiencia muy emocionante.
T: ¿Te gustaría ir a un festival de dos o tres días?
C: Sí, me encantaría ir. Creo que el ambiente sería fantástico. El problema es si hace mal tiempo y llueve todo el tiempo. ¡Sería muy incómodo!
T: ¿Quién es tu cantante favorito? ¿Por qué?
C: Mi cantante favorita es Adele. Tiene una voz fantástica y todo el mundo dice que es muy impresionante verla en directo. Es difícil conseguir entradas porque se venden muy rápidamente.

15. Sport

(a) not having enough time to study
(b) because she would risk failing
(c) she always gets good marks
(d) to switch from going jogging three times a week to playing football

17. Films

(a) they are very exciting, (b) next week

18. TV

(a) lively, (b) all ages, (c) Japan, (d) children aged 8–13

19. Food and drink

Sample answer
C = candidate, T = teacher
T: Usted está en un restaurante de España.
T: ¿En qué puedo servirle?
C: Quiero una mesa para cuatro personas, por favor.
T: Muy bien. ¿Qué quiere comer?
C: Me gustaría la tortilla de patatas y una ensalada mixta.
T: Perfecto. ¿Y para beber?
C: Me gustaría tomar agua mineral.
T: ¿La comida está bien?
C: Sí, me gusta mucho la tortilla. Es deliciosa.
T: Muy bien.
C: ¿Cuánto es en total?
T: Son treinta y ocho euros.

20. Eating in a café

(a) B, (b) B, (c) B, (d) A, (e) A+B

21. Eating in a restaurant

(a) It's a great place where you can eat really well It's quiet.
(b) Colleagues from the office.
(c) Going somewhere else for coffee.
(d) No. There was nobody else there.
(e) It smelled of disinfectant.

22. Meals at home

(a) it tastes better
(b) by being organised
(c) to be interested in the rest of the family

23. Shopping for food

(a) C, (b) B, (c) C

24. Opinions about food

(a) Spanish food
(b) Greek
(c) her favourite food is Greek food

25. Celebrations

Sample answer
Normalmente mis padres me dan mis regalos por la mañana. Por la tarde vamos a cenar a alguno de mis restaurantes favoritos.
La Navidad pasada, mi familia y yo abrimos los regalos primero. Después todos ayudamos a preparar la comida porque mis tíos y mis primos vinieron a comer.
Creo que las celebraciones son importantes porque las familias se reúnen y todos se relajan.
Este fin de semana es el aniversario de mis padres y vamos a tener una fiesta en casa. Habrá música y juegos y mucho para comer y beber.

26. Customs

(a) in big cities
(b) that the siesta increases productivity

27. Spanish festivals

Sample answer
C = Candidate; T = Teacher
T: ¿Que hay en la foto?
C: En esta foto se ve una fiesta tradicional con muchos fuegos artificiales magníficos. En la foto hay mucha gente y parece un espectáculo fantástico. A mí me encantaría ir a esta fiesta.
T: ¿Que piensas de las fiestas?
C: Para mí las fiestas son muy importantes porque nos dan la oportunidad de entender más de la cultura de un lugar y de formar parte de un grupo grande de gente de varias edades. Además son muy divertidas.
T: Describe una fiesta a la que has asistido.
C: El año pasado mi familia y yo fuimos a una fiesta tradicional del pueblo pequeño donde vivo. Se cerraron las calles al tráfico y bailamos mucho.
T: ¿Por qué piensas que hay tantas fiestas en España?
C: Creo que muchas fiestas tienen su origen en la religión porque España es un país católico pero también creo que las fiestas se deben al buen clima. Es mucho más fácil celebrar fiestas y eventos al aire libre cuando hace buen tiempo y no llueve mucho. En mi país hace frío y llueve bastante. Por eso hay pocas fiestas.
T: ¿Qué fiesta española te gustaría ver?
C: A mí me encantaría tener la oportunidad de ir a La Tomatina en España. Me parece una fiesta muy divertida y siempre he querido lanzar tomates a alguien.

28. South American festivals

La corrida de toros es una tradición española que también se celebra en muchos países sudamericanos. El año pasado fui a visitar la plaza de toros en México y vi una corrida. No me gustó nada pero el ambiente fue muy emocionante y fue una nueva experiencia. No iré otra vez.

Local, national, international and global areas of interest

29. Describing a region

(a) Tiene paisajes, pueblos blancos y costas.
(b) Hay (mucha) cultura y tradiciones.

30. Describing a town

D, F, H

31. Places to see

(a) museum shop, (b) chemist's/pharmacy, (c) art gallery, (d) buy bread

32. Places to visit

Sample answer
Se puede visitar el museo y así se conoce la cultura. A mí me encanta Bilbao porque se puede experimentar la cultura vasca. También se puede caminar por el casco antiguo y se puede ver un espectáculo de música vasca porque forma parte de su patrimonio cultural. ¿Usted ha visitado el casco antiguo de Bilbao?

33. The weather

(a) B, (b) A, (c) A

34. Shopping

A

35. Buying gifts

Sample answer

C = candidate, T = teacher

T: Usted está en una tienda de ropa en un pueblo de España y quiere comprar algo.

T: Hola. ¿En qué puedo ayudarle?

C: Me gustaría comprar una gorra.

T: Muy bien. Tenemos varios colores. ¿Cuál prefiere?

C: Prefiero una gorra roja. ¿Cuánto cuesta la gorra?

T: Son veinte euros. Habla bien el español. ¿De dónde es usted?

C: Soy de Escocia.

T: Muy bien. ¿Le gusta este pueblo?

C: Sí, me gusta mucho porque es muy pintoresco y bastante pequeño.

36. Money

(a) to buy a new mobile

(b) buy lots of magazines and books/novels

(c) she's going to work in a hairdresser's

37. Charities

(a) B, (b) C, (c) E

38. Volunteering

(a) communicating with others / improving personal relationships

(b) two years ago

(c) skills / better job prospects

(d) it was incredible / he'd recommend it

39. Helping others

(a) preparar una comida / ir al supermercado

(b) ofrecer hacer de canguro

40. Healthy living

Sample answer

C = Candidate; T = Teacher

T: ¿Qué hay en la foto?

C: En la foto hay una familia que come a la mesa. Es una comida muy sana porque toman una ensalada y diferentes tipos de fruta.

T: ¿Qué haces tú para llevar una vida activa?

C: En mi tiempo libre me gusta hacer deporte y el domingo jugué al tenis con mi hermano. Mañana iré a la piscina porque me encanta la natación. Cuando hago ejercicio, me siento más sana.

T: ¿Qué comida sana comiste ayer?

C: Ayer comí una sopa de verduras y tomé una ensalada de pollo. Bebí un zumo de naranja.

T: ¿Como vas a mejorar tu dieta en el futuro?

C: Voy a evitar la comida con mucha grasa y comeré más fruta. Intentaré limitar el número de caramelos que como. Voy a tomar café sin azúcar.

T: ¿Qué otros aspectos son importantes para tener una vida sana?

C: Es importante dormir bien también y por lo tanto es mejor acostarse a una hora razonable. Así puedes dormir unas ocho horas y tener energía al día siguiente.

41. Unhealthy living

(b) E, (c) A, (d) F

42. Peer group pressure

Sample answer

Mi amiga Laura tiene gafas y es bastante alta. Es una chica muy inteligente, pero a veces es un poco tímida. Para mí una buena amiga debe guardar los secretos y decir la verdad. Gracias a ella empecé a comer más sano y no cedí ante la presión del grupo de beber alcohol o de tomar malas decisiones. En el futuro, Laura y yo vamos a hacer más deporte. Me gustaría aprender a montar a caballo.

43. Green issues

Sample answer

Para mí, el problema más grande es el calentamiento global. Pienso que deberíamos usar más el transporte público y reutilizar más productos.

Es esencial que trabajemos contra la destrucción de la capa de ozono si queremos salvar nuestro planeta. Es necesario que reciclemos más y no deberíamos malgastar electricidad ni consumir tanta energía. Además, es importante que compremos pilas recargables y reutilicemos bolsas de plástico.

44. Natural resources

(a) vendió bolsas de tela

(b) las recogió y las llevó a una empresa de reciclaje

(c) recetas para usar los restos de comida

45. Environmental action

Sample answer

Proteger al medio ambiente es esencial porque estamos destruyendo nuestro planeta. Creo que es muy importante reducir el uso de bolsas de plástico porque tardan años en descomponerse. Si más personas se pusieran a no usar bolsas de plástico, no habría tantos problemas de polución.

Este año, he viajado en bicicleta en vez de ir en autobús o coche y he apagado las luces de mi habitación cada día antes de ir al instituto.

46. Global issues

A

47. Poverty

(a) the lack of clean water

(b) the inequality between rich and poor

(c) the shortage of modern medicines

48. Homelessness

(a) the homeless having nothing to eat at Christmas
(b) an empty shop
(c) a dining room for the needy
(d) soups and hot food
(e) they can keep warm for a while / there will be Christmas spirit

50. Tourist information

… I found out lots of information, like/for example the bus timetable. Tomorrow I will do a walking tour through/around the town/city centre with my parents.

51. Accommodation

Sample answer
C = Candidate; T = Teacher
T: ¿Qué hay en la foto?
C: En esta foto se ve a una familia que está de vacaciones en un camping con su caravana.
T: ¿Qué piensas de las vacaciones en un camping?
C: No me gusta nada pasar las vacaciones en un camping porque siempre es muy incómodo dormir en una tienda. Además, muchas veces los servicios están sucios o las duchas no funcionan.
T: Háblame de la última vez que fuiste de vacaciones.
C: Normalmente voy a un camping bastante aburrido pero el año pasado me quedé en un hotel precioso de cinco estrellas. Tenía una piscina enorme y las habitaciones eran muy limpias y bastante grandes. Me encantan los hoteles lujosos pero el problema es que son muy caros.
T: Qué planes tienes para las vacaciones este año?
C: Este año voy con mi familia a la Costa Brava en el noreste de España. Vamos a alojarnos en un hotel junto a la playa. Voy a nadar en el mar y tomar el sol al lado de la piscina. Visitaremos Barcelona y haremos una excursión a un parque temático también.
T: Háblame de tus vacaciones ideales.
C: Mis vacaciones ideales serían en un país donde se hable español, como México, Cuba o Venezuela. Sé que estos países tienen unas playas hermosas y mucha cultura para conocer. Mi familia y yo pasaríamos quince días en un hotel bonito. Alquilaríamos bicicletas y nos bañaríamos en el mar cada mañana antes de desayunar. Comeríamos mucha fruta tropical y mariscos frescos. Lo pasaríamos genial.

52. Hotels

Sample answer:
C = candidate, T = teacher
T: Usted está en un hotel en España. Está hablando con la recepcionista. Quiere reservar una habitación.
T: Buenos días. ¿En qué puedo servirle?
C: Quiero una habitación doble con ducha, por favor.
T: Muy bien. ¿Para cuántas noches?
C: Me gustaría la habitación para cinco noches.
T: ¿Prefiere una habitación con vistas al mar o a la montaña?
C: Prefiero una habitación con vistas al mar.
T: De acuerdo. ¿Tiene planes para mañana?

C: Sí, vamos a visitar el castillo y luego nos gustaría ir a un restaurante típico.
¿El desayuno está incluido en el precio de la habitación?
T: Sí, está incluido.

53. Camping

(a) need to keep volume as low as possible at all times
(b) bring a sleeping bag and use the rubbish bins

54. Holiday preferences

Sample answer
Mis vacaciones perfectas serían en España con un grupo de amigos del instituto. Podríamos hacer deportes acuáticos y bailar en algunas discotecas.
Cuando estoy de vacaciones, lo que no me gusta hacer es tomar el sol y descansar. Prefiero ser activo y aprender cosas nuevas.
El año pasado, mi familia y yo fuimos a Francia para esquiar y fue fantástico. Me caí mucho el primer día pero fue muy divertido y al final de la semana había aprendido a esquiar en paralelo.
El año que viene voy a montar a caballo con mi hermano porque me encanta la equitación.

56. Travelling

(a) C, (b) B, (c) C

57. Holiday activities

Sample answer
Siempre voy de vacaciones con mi hermana. Tiene dos años más que yo, por lo que tenemos los mismos gustos. El año pasado fuimos a Ibiza. ¡Fue estupendo! Nos bañamos en el mar y descansamos en la playa. Por las noches íbamos a las discotecas y bailábamos hasta las tres de la mañana. Yo creo que a mis padres les gustaría que fuéramos con ellos pero sería aburrido.

58. Holiday experiences

(a) Everything was closed and there was nobody about.
(b) by bus or by bike
(c) speak and understand Arturo's language

59. Transport and directions

(a) better for the environment
(b) catches the bus

60. Transport problems

(a) B, (b) A, (c) D, (d) C, (e) A

61. Holiday problems

(a) waiter is not doing job properly
(b) clean the tables / make sure everything is clean

62. Asking for help abroad

Listen to the recording

TRACK 66

Sample answer
C = candidate, T = teacher
T: Usted está en una comisaría de España denunciando el robo de su monedero.
T: Buenas tardes. ¿Qué ha ocurrido exactamente?
C: Un hombre me ha robado el monedero hace media hora.
T: ¿Dónde ha tenido lugar el robo?
C: Tuvo lugar en el centro comercial, en un café.
T: ¿Puede describir al ladrón?
C: Sí. El ladrón era rubio con el pelo corto y rizado. Era bastante alto.
T: ¿Cómo es su monedero?
C: Es azul marino con rayas blancas.

Current and future study and employment

63. School subjects

(a) IT, (b) Physics, (c) PE, (d) a waste of time

64. Success in school

(a) turn off your mobile
(b) doing homework well / concentrating in class
(c) patience / motivation / tenacity

65. School life

(a) No hablo nunca/Nunca hablo con mis amigos en clase.
(b) A veces leo libros en la biblioteca.
(c) Ayer por la mañana escribí un ensayo de historia.
(d) Prefiero hablar con el profesor/la profesora porque odio copiar de la pizarra.

66. The school day

(a) It only lasts 15 minutes.
(b) It lasts 45 minutes.
(c) He always has a club / activity (after school).

67. Comparing schools

Listen to the recording

TRACK 67

Sample answer
Los colegios en España son diferentes de los colegios ingleses. Los alumnos no llevan uniforme y las clases terminan a las dos. Además, las vacaciones son más largas: casi tres meses. ¡Me gustaría ir al instituto en España!
En Inglaterra los alumnos llevan uniforme y no lo soporto, pero visité un instituto español durante un intercambio y ¡qué sorpresa! Los alumnos españoles no tenían que llevarlo. ¡Qué envidia! ¡No es justo! Lo que más me gusta es que las vacaciones son más largas y por eso preferiría estar en España.

69. School rules

Listen to the recording

TRACK 68

Sample answer
En mi instituto tengo que llevar uniforme. Odio el uniforme porque es incómodo. En mi opinión, las normas son anticuadas. Son tontas e inútiles pero algunas personas piensan que son necesarias. ¡Qué horror!
En mi instituto, hay muchas normas. Acaban de introducir una nueva y ahora no se permite usar el móvil en clase. ¡No es justo! Hay que dejarlo en casa, o apagarlo antes de entrar en el instituto. Creo que los profesores son demasiado estrictos.

70. Problems at school

D, F

72. School trips

(a) A, (b) C, (c) C

73. School events

(a) academic success / pupils going to universities / pupils continuing studying
(b) the play (they have just seen)
(c) the actors / those who helped during the show

74. School exchanges

Listen to the recording

TRACK 69

Sample answer
C = candidate, T = teacher
T: ¿Qué hay en la foto?
C: En esta foto hay un grupo de estudiantes ingleses que ha ido a España para hacer un intercambio. Han visitado el centro histórico de la cuidad.
T: ¿Qué piensas de los intercambios?
C: A mí me encantan los intercambios porque te permiten hacer nuevos amigos de otro país.
T: Describe un intercambio o una excursión cultural de tu instituto.
C: El año pasado estuve con una familia muy amable de Madrid. Aprendí mucho español y fue muy interesante ir al instituto.
T: ¿Adónde te gustaría ir y por qué?
C: En el futuro me gustaría ir a Sudamérica. Quiero aprender más de la cultura latinoamericana.
T: ¿Por qué son importantes los intercambios?
C: Los intercambios son importantes porque nos ayudan a conocer otros países y a dominar otros idiomas.

75. Future plans

Listen to the recording

TRACK 70

Sample answer
Cuando sea mayor y termine la universidad, viajaré mucho. Ganaré mucho dinero así que seré feliz porque podré comprar mucha ropa.

77. Using languages

(a) (2 of:) travel to more than 20 countries / key in world of business / can understand your own language better and learn others more easily
(b) speak Spanish
(c) Chinese
(d) number of speakers will increase to 7.5% (by 2030)

78. Jobs

(a) fireman
(b) he didn't like working at night
(c) waiter
(d) plumber
(e) you can earn a lot of money

79. Opinions about jobs

(a) C, (b) B

80. Applying for jobs

B, E, F

81. Careers and training

Sample answer
T: ¿Qué profesión te gustaría hacer?
C: Como profesión tengo la idea de ser piloto porque me chiflan los aviones, me encanta volar y parece ser una profesión bastante variada.
T: En tu opinión, ¿qué importancia tiene el pago de un trabajo?
C: Creo que es esencial encontrar un trabajo bien pagado si quieres vivir en una ciudad como Londres.

Grammar

82. Nouns and articles

1 (a) folletos   (c) tradiciones   (e) actores
   (b) veces   (d) cafés
2 (a) la, (b) el (c) el, (d) la, (e) la

83. Adjectives

pequeña, bonitas, ingleses, simpática, habladora, históricos, ruidosos, interesantes
Translation answer:
Mallorca is a small island. It has many beautiful beaches. In Mallorca there are lots of English tourists. People there are very kind and very talkative. Mallorca has lots of historical museums and a lot of noisy bars. You can do lots of interesting things.

84. Possessives and pronouns

mi, sus, mi, que, su, el mío, él, el suyo
Translation answer:
My stepfather is called Miguel. His daughters are my stepsisters. My stepsister, who is called Isabel, has a boyfriend, Pablo. Her boyfriend is less handsome than mine. I have been going out with him for six years. Isabel has been going out with hers for a month.

85. Comparisons

1 el peor   5 la mejor
2 los mejores   6 el más feo
3 la más bonita   7 más guapo
4 aburridísimo   8 más perezosa

86. Other adjectives

1 Ese chico es tonto.
2 Esta manzana está rica.
3 Quiero comprar esos vaqueros.
4 Aquella casa es grandísima.
5 Esta película es aburrida.
6 No quiero ese jersey – quiero aquello cárdigan.

87. Pronouns

1 Voy a darlo a mi padre / Lo voy a dar a mi padre.
2 Nunca le escribo.
3 Voy a comprarlo / Lo voy a comprar.
4 Ponlos en la bolsa.
5 Quiero decirle un secreto.

88. The present tense

1 escucho – I don't listen to classical music.
2 hablan – My parents speak English.
3 juega – My friend plays basketball with me.
4 quieres – Do you want to go to the cinema with me tonight?
5 comemos – We always eat fruit to be healthy.
6 encuentran – They always find money in the street.
7 vivís – Do you live in the countryside?
8 duerme – My brother sleeps in his own room.

89. Reflexive verbs (present)

1 Me   3 me   5 te
2 se   4 Nos   6 se

90. Irregular verbs (present)

1 salgo – I leave at 7.30 to go to the concert.
2 tienen – My cousins have blue eyes and they are blond.
3 sé – I really like to go/going to the beach but I don't know how to swim.
4 cojo – I always take the bus when I go to school.
5 hacen, hago – My friends do their homework in the library but I do it at home.
6 conduzco – I think that I drive very well but my father does not think so!

91. *Ser* and *estar*

1 está   3 es   5 son   7 están
2 es   4 estoy   6 es   8 está

92. The gerund

1 Estoy / Estaba jugando al tenis.
2 Estoy / Estaba escribiendo un correo electrónico.
3 Está / Estaba hablando con mi amigo Juan.
4 Está / Estaba durmiendo en la cama.
5 Estoy / Estaba comiendo cereales.
6 Estoy / Estaba tomando el sol en la playa.
7 Están / Estaban navegando por Internet.
8 ¿Estás / ¿Estabas cantando en tu habitación?

93. The preterite tense

1 I go to Italy. (present)
2 I arrived at six. (preterite)
3 I surf the internet. (present)
4 He / She listened to music. (preterite)
5 He / She went to a party which was great. (preterite)
6 It was cold and it rained a bit. (preterite)
7 We saw Pablo in the market. (preterite)
8 I played basketball on the beach. (preterite)

94. The imperfect tense

1	trabajaba	3	iba	5	visité
2	comí	4	había	6	lloraba

95. The future tense

1 (a) Nunca fumaré.
   (b) Ayudaré a los demás .
   (c) Cambiaremos el mundo.
   (d) Trabajaré en un aeropuerto.
2 (a) Voy a salir a las seis.
   (b) Voy a ser médico.
   (c) Va a ir a España.
   (d) Mañana voy a jugar al tenis.

96. The conditional tense

bebería, haría, practicaría, tomaría, bebería, comería, me acostaría, dormiría, llevaría

97. Perfect and pluperfect

1 He visitado Palma con mi novio. (perfect)
2 Han hecho sus deberes con mi ayuda. (perfect)
3 Habíamos ido al supermercado con Pablo. (pluperfect)
4 Mi hermana ha escrito una carta de amor. (perfect)
5 ¿Has visto mi abrigo? (perfect)
6 Cuando llegó, mis primos habían comido ya. (pluperfect)

98. Giving instructions

1 Write to me.
2 Wait for your sister.
3 Don't tell me anything.
4 Don't shout!
5 Click here.
6 Don't take photos!
7 Answer the questions.
8 Don't leave everything to the last minute.

99. The present subjunctive

1 When I go to university, I'll study French.
2 I don't think your friend is good-looking.
3 When I'm 18, I'll take a gap year.
4 I want you to talk to Pablo.
5 It's not true that English food is horrible.
6 I don't think Italy is the best football team.

100. Negatives

Suggested answers:
1 No como nunca verduras.
2 No tengo ningún libro.
3 No conozco a nadie.
4 Nadie juega al baloncesto. / No juega nadie al baloncesto.
5 Nunca hago mis deberes. / No hago nunca mis deberes.
6 No me gusta ni navegar por Internet ni descargar música.
7 No tiene nada.
8 No tengo ningún amigo en Londres.

Translation answers:
1 I always eat vegetables.
2 I have a book.
3 I know all (of) his / her friends.
4 Everyone plays basketball.
5 I always do my homework.
6 I like to surf the internet and download music.
7 It / He / She has everything.
8 I have lots of friends in London.

101. Special verbs

1	Me duele	5	Le duelen
2	Le gusta	6	Me encanta
3	Me gustaron	7	Nos quedan
4	Les hace falta	8	A María le gustan

102. *Por* and *para*

1 (a) para, (b) para, (c) por, (d) para, (e) para, (f) por, (g) por
2 (a) para, (b) por, (c) para, (d) por, (e) ✓, (f) para, (g) ✓, (h) ✓

103. Questions and exclamations

1	d	3	h	5	a	7	c
2	f	4	e	6	b	8	g

104. Connectives and adverbs

1 *Suggested answers:*
   (a) Nunca voy a Paris porque es aburrido.
   (b) Mientras jugaba al baloncesto, Juan hacía patinaje.
   (c) Después de estudiar, iré a la universidad.
   (d) Nos gustaría ir a la playa pero está lloviendo.
2 (a) tranquilamente (peacefully)
   (b) perfectamente (perfectly)
   (c) difícilmente (with difficulty)
   (d) severamente (strictly)

105. Numbers

1 las nueve menos veinte
2 cuatrocientos sesenta y cinco
3 el doce de junio de dos mil catorce
4 séptimo
5 las once y media
6 setenta y seis
7 el primero / el uno de enero de mil novecientos noventa y siete
8 tercero

Vocabulary

117. Internet and social media

1 Me gusta chatear en línea con mis amigos por la tarde.
2 El ciberacoso no es un problema en mi instituto.
3 Quiero ser programador cuando deje el instituto.

Published by Pearson Education Limited, 80 Strand, London, WC2R 0RL.

www.pearsonschoolsandfecolleges.co.uk

Text and illustrations © Pearson Education Limited 2017
Typeset and illustrated by Kamae Design, Oxford
Produced by Out of House Publishing
Cover illustration by Miriam Sturdee

The right of Vivien Halksworth to be identified as author of this work has been asserted by her in accordance with the Copyright, Designs and Patents Act 1988.

First published 2017

20
10 9 8 7

British Library Cataloguing in Publication Data
A catalogue record for this book is available from the British Library

ISBN 9781292131443

Printed in Great Britain by Bell and Bain Ltd, Glasgow

Acknowledgements
Content written by Ian Kendrick and Leanda Reeves is included.

The author and publisher would like to thank the following individuals and organisations for permission to reproduce material:
Page 71 Save the Children logo. Used with the permission of Save the Children.

Photographs
(Key: b-bottom; c-centre; l-left; r-right; t-top)

123RF.com: 80, Sanchai khudpin 73; **Alamy Stock Photo:** Cultura Creative 44c, Eddie Gerald 27, Johner Images 44cr, Neil Juggins 45cr, Newzulu 26, Picture Partners 69, Pixoi Ltd 79l; **Fotolia.com:** alekseykh 35cr, auremar 91b, flairimages 51, Monkey Business 64, paul_brighton 74r, Picture-Factory 60, Sergiy Bykhunenko 20; **Getty Images:** Thomas Barwick 21; **Pearson Education Ltd:** Jules Selmes 102cl, MindStudio 84cl, 84cr, 84br, 85, Sophie Bluy 4, 12, 67, 79r, 86, Studio 8 83, 87, Tudor Photography 35r; **Shutterstock.com:** Ahturner 40tr, Darren Blake 95, debr22pics 102cr, Diego Grandi 28, Fedor Selivanov 44tr, Goran Djukanovic 14, grafvision 76, Ieva Vincer 48, jan kranendonk 74l, John Wollwerth 47, Joshua Haviv 93, Karramba Production 78, Monkey Business Images 81, Morgan Lane Photography 43, photobank.ch 45tr, PhotoBarmaley 50, RamonaS 91t, Spotmatik Ltd 40cr, Syda Productions 41

All other images © Pearson Education

Note from the publisher
Pearson has robust editorial processes, including answer and fact checks, to ensure the accuracy of the content in this publication, and every effort is made to ensure this publication is free of errors. We are, however, only human, and occasionally errors do occur. Pearson is not liable for any misunderstandings that arise as a result of errors in this publication, but it is our priority to ensure that the content is accurate. If you spot an error, please do contact us at resourcescorrections@pearson.com so we can make sure it is corrected.